In Spite of Plato

In Spite of Plato

A Feminist Rewriting of Ancient Philosophy

Adriana Cavarero
Foreword by Rosi Braidotti

Translated by
Serena Anderlini-D'Onofrio and Áine O'Healy

Polity Press

This translation copyright © Polity Press 1995
First published in Italian as *Nonostante Platone: Figure femminili nella filosofia antica* copyright © Editori Riuniti 1990.
This translation first published 1995 by Polity Press in association with Blackwell Publishers Ltd.

Editorial office:
Polity Press
65 Bridge Street
Cambridge CB2 1UR, UK

Marketing and production:
Blackwell Publishers Ltd
108 Cowley Road
Oxford OX4 1JF, UK

ISBN 0 7456-1259-8
ISBN 0 7456-1572-4 (pbk)

A CIP catalogue record for this book is available from the British Library.

Typeset in Sabon on 11/13 pt
by Colset Pte Ltd Singapore

Printed in Great Britain by Hartnolls Ltd., Bodmin, Cornwall

This book is printed on acid-free paper.

Contents

Acknowledgements

The author, translator and publishers wish to thank the following who have kindly given permission for the use of copyright material.

Arsenale Editrice srl for Bianca Tarozzi, 'Variazioni sul tema di Penelope' from *Nessuno vince il leone*, 1989, p.21;

Every effort has been made to trace all the copyright holders but if any have been inadvertently overlooked the publishers will be pleased to make the necessary arrangement at the first opportunity.

Foreword by
Rosi Braidotti

It is a privilege to introduce the first translation into English of a book-length work by Adriana Cavarero. As some of her articles have already been translated in recent anthologies of Italian feminist theory and in other international publications,[1] the translation of this book is a timely and important event.

Cavarero is one of Italy's most prominent ancient philosophy specialists and she is by far the most important feminist philosopher of sexual difference in that country. She is Senior Lecturer in political philosophy at the University of Verona and has a distinguished list of publications in the field of ancient Greek philosophy as well as in modern political thought, especially Hobbes, Locke, and social contract theory.

For Cavarero, as for most philosophers trained at her *alma mater*, the University of Padua, philosophy is grounded in the texts of the classical tradition which, beginning with antiquity, reaches all the way through to the German Hegelian tradition. Her interest in Marxism, in the tradition of Gramsci's materialism, and in political theory in general also stems from this source. Throughout her career, Cavarero has been closely linked to left-wing theories and political movements. In addition she has played an active role in prestigious research groups, such as the Gramsci Institute (Venice), and the journals *Il Centauro* (Padua) and *Il Mulino* (Bologna); she is also a member of the editorial board of *Filosofia e politica*, which focuses on the history of a European political lexicon.

Cavarero's intellectual and theoretical itinerary is thoroughly embedded within the Italian left: she has played an important role in the executive committees of the former Communist Party (PCI) and of the contemporary Democratic Party of the Left (PDS), especially on issues related to the status of women and to sexual difference as a political practice. She contributes regularly to left-wing newspapers such as *L'Unità* and *Il Manifesto*.

Cavarero's involvement in the women's movement is long-standing. She was a founding member of the feminist philo-sophical community "Diotima," which works within the University of Verona, and has strong links with the Milan women's bookshop.[2] Since 1991, however, Cavarero has worked more closely with the community-based group "Il Filo di Arianna."[3]

I shall not conceal the fact that this introduction is also a pretext that allows me to continue the intellectual dialogue that I have been fortunate enough to establish with Cavarero about feminist philosophy over the years of meeting, of conference papers,[4] and of intense personal correspondence. This high level of interaction expresses in a very concrete manner the political and theoretical practice of woman-to-woman dialogue which is central to the project of sexual difference.

Although Adriana Cavarero's work is eminently philosophical and it has received widespread recognition in Italian academic culture and society, Cavarero is free of that special brand of corporatism that seems to mark so many philosophers – male and female. Cavarero's work is centered on a feminist deconstruction of the metaphysical tradition in Western philosophy and, to that effect, it displays a very imaginative and yet rigorous brand of interdisciplinarity. Of special relevance to her style are the references to literary sources and to moral and especially political problems and issues, of which readers will find ample evidence in this book.

The author's research on Ancient Greek philosophy is consequently not the aim, but rather the starting point for a critical reflection that touches upon contemporary concerns and issues. Similarly, Cavarero's feminist concerns have a double edge which makes them relevant both to women's struggles and the feminist community and also to a broader spectrum of critical activities. Her work has always struck me as marked by a yearning for a radical, woman-centered redefinition of the human. In this project, philosophy plays the role of a privileged, if limited, instrument of analysis: it is an honorable and beloved tool-box. I therefore think that what is at stake in Cavarero's philosophical approach is not only the legitimation of feminist knowledge claims but also the question of the relevance and the range of social and political applications of philosophy itself.

Loyal to the methodological premises of the feminist poststructuralist philosopher Luce Irigaray, who is one of her main feminist sources of inspiration, Cavarero considers metaphysics as the foundation stone of Western theoretical language. This means that the metaphysical tradition cannot be considered as just any branch of philosophy, but rather as its central axis of discursive power. This strategic position makes it urgent for feminists and other critical thinkers to elaborate relevant critiques of the metaphysical structure of philosophical thought.

What I wish to suggest here is that, from her very early writings,[5] and through to her more recent theoretical developments,[6] Cavarero has been able to strike a difficult balance between two potentially conflicting tendencies within her thought; on the one hand, her reliance on the metaphysical tradition, which she deconstructs through a feminist analysis of the role it has played in legitimating patriarchal power; on the other hand, her determination to undermine this tradition, mostly thanks to her subversive technique of reading philosophy through the grid of sexual difference.

It might be tempting for the English-speaking reader to interpret this problem in terms of the contemporary debate on modernity versus postmodernity. In Cavarero's work, this could be rendered as, on the one hand, an attachment to the rationalist bedrock of Western philosophy and, on the other, a healthy dose of skepticism about the self-regulating capacity of rationality. I do think, however, that there is not much to be gained by classifying Cavarero's work in such a manner. The modern-versus-postmodern debate has become a massive, vulgarized affair, even in feminist circles; thus, to do justice to the depth and originality of Cavarero's work, the reader would have to study carefully how the label "postmodern" functions in Italian intellectual and political contexts. Italy has developed a strong school of postmodernism, which is probably most evident in the field of architecture and the arts. The critical work of Giuliana Bruno in these fields is well known to English-speaking readers.[7] Italian philosophy has responded with an equally impressive trend to postmodern thinking, which is significantly called "il pensiero debole" ("weak thought"). Philosophers such as Massimo Cacciari – newly elected progressive mayor of the city of Venice, Gianni Vattimo, and Franco Rella, to mention only a few, are leading intellectual and social figures in contemporary Italian society. They are also of the same generation as Adriana Cavarero and are her friends and colleagues.

The reader would be amazed to discover how many of the path-breaking philosophical discussions that were to change the shape of Italian philosophy, politics, and feminism actually took place on the famous railroad line that runs from Venice to Turin, via Padua, Verona, and Milan. In some ways, this rail-track traces one, enormously influential, line of progressive thinking right across the northern edge of the peninsula. It was at the western end that Adriana Cavarero went to school, completing her secondary education in a *liceo classico* (grammar school) that is a national monument of anti-fascist resistance, having produced people of the calibre of Cesare Pavese, Leone Ginzburg, Giulio Einaudi, and Norberto Bobbio. The young Cavarero came to maturity in the shadow of what can only be described as the giants of Italy's post-war progressive generation.

At the eastern end, between Venice and Verona, Cavarero was to fulfill her own historical role in the complex and often tormented political climate of Italy in the 1970s. The reader needs to keep in mind phenomena that are specific to Italian political culture, such as the size and influence of the former Communist party. Of great significance are also events such as the armed rebellion of terrorist groups, which were centered on Padua though they operated throughout the country, and the great state repression that finally managed to contain them, if not to suppress them altogether. Though the Italian feminist movement as a whole rejected political violence, it was deeply affected by this intense climate and, partly in reaction to it, developed a much stronger sense of the positive force of women's own political traditions and strategies. Cavarero played a leading role in this effort.

What seems absolutely clear to me is that, in such a context, the "modern-versus-postmodern" debate really requires some important readjustments, if it is to make sense at all. Unlike her friend and fellow-commuter[8] Cacciari, who fully embraced the weakened epistemology of deconstruction, and in clear opposition to Bobbio's attachment to the Enlightenment project, Cavarero strikes a different speaking stance: one in which feminism plays a foundational role.

Though she denies anything like an epistemological break in post-modernity, Cavarero both recognizes and makes her work accountable for some of the central paradoxes of what I can only call, following Jean-François Lyotard, "the postmodern condition". First and foremost among them is the question of how to rethink subjectivity and sexual difference. Cavarero therefore invites us not to be easily seduced by the mirage of a "feminized" postmodern male philosophy; it is not the case that the postmodern condition *per se* is an answer to the feminist struggle. Rather, women must track down the complicity between postmodernism and patriarchal assumptions about woman-as-other.

The result is a productive kind of paradox: while taking critical distance from "male-stream" postmodernism, Cavarero elaborates a set of ideas and a philosophical style which are thoroughly relevant to the question of how to solve the postmodern crisis. It is this fragile yet rigorously defended balance between paradoxical positions that makes Cavarero's work so interesting because it gives her great freedom of thought. Her strategic moves within and beyond the canon of Western metaphysics allow her to both state the continuity between classical philosophy and postmodern thought and to activate a qualitative gap between this tradition and feminist political and theoretical practice.

Cavarero's stated intention is to legitimate the role women can play in philosophical discourses and more especially to inscribe sexual difference at the heart of the phallogocentric code that sustains the male symbolic system. That the short-term impact of this position should be a renewal of interest in philosophy itself by women as a group of relative latecomers into this discipline is another revealing paradox. Cavarero's work has an immediate empowering effect upon women philosophers and, as such, I take it as evidence of the dissonance which exists between feminist and mainstream philosophers when it comes to the alleged "crisis" of philosophy as a master discourse. In reaction to the same historical conditions, feminists and male philosophers react quite differently: whereas the latter tend to give in to a melancholic discourse about loss and decline, the former display both an enthusiasm worthy of neophytes and the energy and imagination that I tend to associate with feminism.

Cavarero turns the paradoxes of her position as a female feminist philosopher into a strength by developing a style of philosophical thought that suits both the complexity of her postmodern historical location and the steadfastness of her feminism.

In this book, for instance, Cavarero presents us with a careful rewriting of some of the central figures in Greek philosophy, such as they appear in Plato's texts and in surrounding myths: Penelope, the Thracian maidservant, Demeter, and Diotima. Emphasizing the importance of these figures not only as textual characters but also as key-elements in the conceptual structure of Plato's thought, Cavarero works through them and opens them up to a series of non-canonical readings. The method consists in stripping these figures of their successive layers of possible interpretation, like the many skins of an onion, to quote the unforgettable image proposed by Roland Barthes.

By means of this textual strategy, Cavarero returns the female figures in the classical texts to their literal, as opposed to their metaphorical, significance: she reads them as a woman reading women-in-the-text. Through this process, Cavarero establishes a web of interconnections between the representation of women in classical texts and the practice of sexual difference. Perfectly aware of the fact that these characters are the invention of male authors and that therefore they cannot be taken at face value as the expression of a female voice, Cavarero nonetheless claims that female readers do make a difference to the reception of these textual female figures. She thus takes a position that avoids romanticizing or essentializing the feminine, while asserting the powerful transformative presence of women. Between the feminist woman reader and the woman in the text there is a relation of identification and recognition: both are caught in a masculine conceptual universe. The active presence of female feminist readers is the factor that can alter the reception and therefore also the political usefulness of Plato's texts.

Through her subtle scholarly readings of female figures in these texts, Cavarero makes a strong intervention in contemporary feminist theory. Claiming that these female characters emanating from man-authored texts can and indeed should be reappropriated by today's feminist readers, the author also states that this strategy of repossession can provide new fuel for the feminist debate on women's subjectivity. Avoiding carefully the trap of gyno-centric readings, Cavarero turns this strategy into one of purposeful and deliberate conceptual theft: she steals back from the patriarchal imaginary female figures that then get turned to other uses and purposes. Akin to the great writer and theorist of *écriture féminine* Hélène Cixous, whose work, however, has had little or no influence in Italy, she practices a merry version of conceptual pickpocketing as a creative feminist gesture.

Cavarero suggests that this kind of reappropriation is made necessary by the state of symbolic poverty and theoretical absence to which women have been confined in Western philosophical thought. In other words, precisely because there is no canon other than the masculine one and because even the few female figures that are available in texts are the creation of man, Cavarero proposes that feminist readers of today reappropriate these figures and reread them in the light of their experience. We thus end up with embodied feminist subjects revisiting the textual site of feminine figures, and walking off with new knowledge claims and meanings.

Repossessing them means that the author proceeds to activate these textual figures by playing them off against her own experience and her sense of some of the most urgent problems facing today's women. For instance, the question of motherhood as both experience and institution, which is symbolized by Demeter, is literally the pre-text to a series of reflections on the role of the mother in contemporary biotechnologies and bioethics. Once again, Cavarero avoids nostalgic longings for a matriarchal order, while evoking in lyrical language the traces of a lost female community, buried under a historical system of male domination.

Central to Cavarero's project is the desire to transcend patriarchal dualism and to reintegrate the subject in a continuum of mind and body, starting from a radical redefinition of women's relation to the mother. In this regard, following Irigaray, Cavarero traces both a historical account of phallocentric thought and also the itinerary of female transcendence from it. I would define this as Cavarero's own brand of mimetic strategy, which is a subversive political move inspired by Luce Irigaray's work.

I think it is important at this stage to clarify the extraordinary role played by Luce Irigaray in Italian feminist politics and in Cavarero's own work. Contrary to the English reception of Irigaray's work – which was belated (*Speculum*, published in 1974, was translated into English in 1985) and highly controversial – Irigaray met with instant recognition in Italian culture and especially within the women's movement. Her works have been almost simultaneously translated from the very beginning, with key feminist figures like Luisa Muraro and Adriana Cavarero playing a leading role in getting Irigaray's idea of sexual difference recognized as a fundamental political theory.

I think this is the point where the Italian reception of Irigaray's work differs the most from the English-language one: in Italy, she was recognized as a leading political philosopher who was bent upon redefining the terms of political subjectivity by exposing the deeply sexed nature of the state, the notion of citizenship, and the entitlements they represent. Contrary to "standpoint" feminists who go on beleiving in the self-redeeming properties of the system's political rationality, Irigaray insisted on the need for an in-depth revolution of the socio-symbolic structures on which the system rests. This made her a crucial national figure in Italy, where she has served as adviser to the PDS and to women's organizations for years. While this process of forging a link between her philosophy and concrete political practices was going on, the English-language debate about her work got bogged down in the highly inflated and thoroughly misleading debate against "essentialism," to which I shall return shortly.

In this respect, Italian feminism provides us with a highly instructive laboratory of ideas, where a deeply politicized local women's movement intesects with very complex and sophisticated theoretical frameworks, to produce an exciting forum for both political and theoretical practice.[9]

It should be clear by now that Cavarero's work implies a political understanding of the feminist project, which could not be further removed from an essentialistic understanding of "woman." Cavarero posits the active involvement of real-life, "embodied" female subjects as a factor that makes the difference in the reception of the texts. As Teresa de Lauretis has pointed out,[10] there is an "essential difference" at work here, which is deeply anti-essentialistic. For Cavarero, this strategy of a systematic and politically motivated repossession is in fact a "symbolic" revolution, in that it brings about the affirmation of the positivity of the difference that women can make.

Central to this project, as to all the Italian current of sexual difference, is the political emphasis on the fundamental dissymmetry between the sexes. This implies that the masculine symbolic system – phallocentrism – cannot adequately represent women's experience. That female feminist readers should make a difference proves the extent to which this dissymmetry can become a factor of empowerment for women.

I would define Cavarero as a neo-materialist thinker who situates the female embodied condition at the center of her concerns. What does Cavarero's materialism consist of? In the carefully monitored theft described above; in a willful displacement of the classical teleological route of thought; in a carefully planned derailing of the patriarchal train of thought.

All this, expressed with great elegance, in a style that combines rigor and Latinate lexical terms, with great lyrical force. Cavarero combines scholarly erudition with great skills as a writer, in a manner that is typical of Continental philosophers. Part of the force of this book is due precisely to the charge of its imagination and the poetic resonance of its language. Even in her writing, Cavarero practices a sort of stylistic transdisciplinarity and I think that the excellent translation does justice to the quality of her writing.

By her own admission, Cavarero's writing is a direct application of the strategy of mimetic repetition. She questions the patriarchal order by trying to locate the traces of the feminine as a site of male projection but also as a site of feminist reappropriation of alternative figurations for female subjectivity. Of central importance to the whole project is the redefinition of motherhood and the maternal function, which, far from being reduced to a support of patriarchy, is turned into a structuring or foundational site for the empowerment of women.

Following Irigaray, Cavarero locates in the symbolic underrating of motherhood one of the keys of patriarchal power. Masculine appropriation of the central symbolic functions in Western culture is thus read as a complex form of compensation for the fact that everyone, and that means every man, is of woman born. Adrienne Rich's work has been extremely influential in Italy and it has fed into a theory of "womb envy," or envy for the female matrix, which is one of the pillars of the practice of sexual difference. Recognizing the symbolic debt toward the mother emerges as one of the options available to men. That men – in Italy as everywhere else – seem rather reluctant to accept this debt, reducing the mother to either a social function or a demographic necessity, leaves unresolved the entire question of men in feminism.

This emphasis on the importance of symbolic recognition of the mother does not, however, result in glorification. Adriana Cavarero is a deeply secular thinker, who takes her distance from the more recent developments in Irigaray's thought concerning the necessity of a woman-centered system of mediation to and representation of the divine. There is no alternative theology or counter-metaphysics in Cavarero's work, but only a sustained and systematic effort to negotiate an alternative symbolic representation of women. Very situated in the *hic et nunc* of theoretical praxis, Cavarero carefully explores different models of ethical relationship to "others," starting from the primordial m/other figure, which acts as the threshold of ethical subjectivity.

In this book, she presents several different figurations for man's "others": from woman, the privileged other or "second sex," to the divine or sacred as "vertical" other; without neglecting the animal; the artificial, the technological, as well as the banal everyday objects, as sites of powerful and questioning "otherness." This renewal of attention for "otherness" has important implications for Cavarero's critique of philosophy as a disciplinary field.

Cavarero reminds us of that which centuries of logocentrism tried to negate, namely that there is no conceptual purity. There exists instead a pre-discursive moment in philosophy. There is a moment, which is also a space, which makes possible the closure of philosophical discourse, acting as the silent substratum on which the philosophical *logos* erects itself. Prior to thought and thinking, there is life and there is the living being. This living entity becomes a subject by entry into the symbolic system, which entails the inscription into a cultural code. What Cavarero wishes to stress is that the living being in any case precedes the inscription into the symbolic and thus is prior to its specific order.

Cavarero joins forces with Irigaray here, in the pursuit of a female-sexed materialism which functions as the substratum of and is prior to the phallogocentric order. The distinguishing feature of phallocracy is precisely the fact that it negates, denies, and willfully obliterates the feminine, appropriating entirely the process of making meaning. Instead of recognizing the embodied, sexed, and corporeal nature of the living beings, phallocratic thinking replaces the maternal origin with the highly abstract notion of man being at the origin of himself. This is a cerebral reappropriation of origin by man, which condemns the feminine to a subsidiary position of necessarily silenced other.

Evidence of this is the ancient saying that defines man as the thinking animal, mortal and endowed with language. You find here, according to Cavarero, the central programme of phallogocentrism: the masculinization of the site of origin of the subject and the reduction of masculinity to an abstraction.

In a radical perspective, inspired by her reading of Hannah Arendt's notion of birth and of the natal experience, the author develops the maternal instance as a major factor of sexual difference. Of course, this revalorization is culture-specific and does not refer to the classical texts of the English-speaking debate on motherhood, and it is especially devoid of reference to "the ethics of care" about which so much ink has been spilled. Cavarero instead bases her discussion of the mother as a symbolic figure on the politics of sexual difference. She thus draws attention to the fact that the actual absence of reference to the mother in the classical texts of Greek philosophy is offset by the vast importance attributed to mortality and death in the same texts of this tradition.

We get thus a juxtaposition of emphasis on life and on death within the Western patriarchal order; this dependence on Thanatos can also be explained as a denial of women's generative maternal force. Given that phallogocentrism rests on a death-based worldview. One of the things at stake in feminism is how to reconnect thought and life in a positive manner.

Cavarero thus attacks the solipsistic fantasy of masculine self-generation which lies at the heart of the Western metaphysical tradition and she argues passionately for a new socio-sexual arrangement between the sexes, based on mutual recognition and empowerment. An important step in this direction is to put an end to the symbolic matricide which the phallogogentric system perpetuates through its social, symbolic, and linguistic codes, every time it associates the masculine with the generic term for the human. Cavarero stresses that this is neither the best nor the only available option for our culture and that there are better ways of going about it.

In a mixture of rigor and humor, Cavarero suggests that the metaphysical closure could be replaced by the recognition of the respect due to the infinite singularity of each and everyone.

A combination of multiplicity and interconnection, which defies easy dichotomies and allows for other voices, echoes, and traces to emerge: from the silent yet persistent noise of Penelope's loom, to the laughter of the Thracian maidservant, Cavarero evokes as well as theorizes a strong female presence which is not one, but manifold; not unified, but in process; not essentialized, but politically empowered. Traces of a female presence act as the instigator of a process of political awakening by women, of which today's feminism is only the latest historical manifestation. Always already on the margins of Plato's ideal city, and cheerfully but stubbornly in spite of it.

Translators' Note

One of the key words that created difficulties in translation was the term *sessuazione*, and its adjectival forms *sessuato/a*. *Sessuazione* is a central category of Italian feminist discourse that historically has a similar function to the English category of gender. However, *sessuazione* encompasses the biological concept of sex within the larger category of cultural gender, rather than functioning as its binary opposite. Hence its strong deconstructive potential within Anglophone feminist discourse. To convey this potential, we relied on the context in which the category operates, and chose a variety of terms to render it. Generally, we translate the noun as "sexedness" and the adjective as "sexed," although we have also used the term "sexual difference." A number of options such as "gender" and "sexual identity" might have provided more "readable" solutions. But in general these terms belie the ideological complexity of *sessuazione*. We have used them only when the focus was on the more specifically biological aspects of gender difference.

Since Italian, like French, does not offer separate equivalents for the English terms "female" and "feminine," the adjective *femminile* has traditionally been translated as either "female" or "feminine," depending on the context. Usually (though not always), "female" designates biological difference, and "feminine" most often refers to the cultural construction of that difference. Although the adjective *femmina* exists in Italian, it is much more limited in usage than the English "female," and applies primarily to the gender of animals or human infants. Following the debates on essentialism and on the cultural construction of femininity, there is currently a certain degree of nervousness in Anglophone discourse around the use of the terms "female" and "feminine." Feeling that the tensions on which Cavarero focuses are elsewhere, we have allowed ourselves a certain flexibility in translating the adjective *femminile*, opting for "female" in some contexts, "feminine" in others, and "women's" when this solution seemed more appropriate.

Intero singolare is an innovative phrase Caverero uses to indicate an individual human person. In the original text this phrase seems to have the function of displacing and replacing the concept of the individual, a concept that may be seen as inherently masculine and Western. *Intero singolare* emphasizes the transient quality of a person's life and the relatedness of this life to the collective life of the human species. In Western discourse, the individual is often perceived as a self-contained, independent, and necessary entity. The expression *intero singolare* revises this concept as follows: the individual is a whole (*intero*) of mind and body, whose existence is temporary. S/he is a unique and unrepeatable (*singolare*) moment of being in the larger, ever-changing collective life. Faced with the impossibility of finding a phrase that would literally translate the concepts encapsulated in *intero singolare*, we allow most of the deconstructive force of Cavarero's phrase to be conveyed by the context in which it occurs. In the majority of cases we opt for either "individual human" or "human person."

One of the key concepts that created problems in the translation is *sottrarsi*. *Sottrarsi* is the infinitive of the reflexive form of the verb *sottrarre*, to withdraw. In the phrase *il sottrarsi* this infinitive is used as a noun, with the literal meaning of withdrawing oneself. The category is part of Cavarero's strategy of undermining patriarchal discourse by retrieving the feminine. It operates on several levels. One is mere acknowledgment of the place the social order assigns to the feminine. Another level emphasizes the action of transforming this place into a space where new feminist strategies can be forged. A third level offers philosophical speculation on the possibilities for generating a new logic from this different rhetoric. We use "seclusion," "withdrawal," and "disinvestment" depending on which level is emphasized in the context.

Serena Anderlini-D'Onofrio is a writer, teacher, scholar, and critic who focuses on women and their works. She holds a Ph.D. in Comparative Literature from the University of California, Riverside (1987) and the title of Dottore in Ricerca from the Ministry of Public Education in Rome, Italy (1989). Serena taught modern drama at Vanderbilt University in Nashville, Tennessee, for three years and has been an independent scholar since 1991. She teaches part-time at the University for Humanistic Studies in Solana Beach, California. Serena's first publications on women and theater appeared in *Feminist Issues*, *Diacritics*, *Leggere Donna*, *Theater*, *The Journal of American Theater and Drama* and *The Journal of Dramatic Theory and Criticism*. She is also a contributor to *Feminine Feminists* (University of Minnesota Press, 1994).

Áine O'Healy is Associate Professor of Italian and Director of European Studies at Loyola Marymount University in Los Angeles. She is the author of *Cesare Pavese* (Boston, 1988) and of numerous articles on contemporary Italian literature and cinema.

Introduction

Western culture is replete with mythic figures that provide a self-representation of the symbolic order from which this culture is woven. The process can be traced back to ancient mythology, and can be found in all kinds of literary documents down through the ages, even in the modern period, or rather, in the modern reappropriation of more ancient figures. In the beginning were the gods of Greek myth, then Homer's Odysseus and Polyphemus, then Oedipus in classical tragedy, not to mention the figures in the Bible. Later came Faust and Don Juan, or we could even add Cyrano and Werther.

In fact, the mythic figure has the power to express in a concentrated way the symbolic order that shapes it. Indeed it is within the symbolic order that the figure takes on a signifying name (a proper name). It does this with a kind of immediate, story-like allusiveness, coming to life in a vital, paradigmatic way. Clearly, the symbolic order finds expression in other types of language, for example in philosophical treatises or legal documents (to limit ourselves to the field of the written word). But the mythic figure is incomparable both in its communicative force and in its capacity to stir up a sense of self-recognition. It has an incomparable ability to adapt to the twists and turns of the inner development of the symbolic order itself, like a living character whose different traits gradually become visible from various points of view that evolve over time. Hence we have Freud's Oedipus, Adorno's Ulysses, and Kierkegaard's Don Juan. Within the historical development of this same symbolic order (which shaped its own patriarchal imprint at the very beginning) these different perspectives have unfolded one after the other.

The symbolic framework that supports the hermeneutical system remains the same, despite the representational polyvalence of the mythic figures deployed within it *ad infinitum*. Here, a male subject claiming to be neutral/universal declares his central position, disseminating a sense of the world cut to his own measure and revealed in his own mythic figures. According to this perspective, even female figures have a place *in reference* to the male subject who is at the origin of their creation. For Zeus there is Hera, for Odysseus Penelope, for Faust Gretchen, for Don Giovanni Zerlina, and many others. But the couple, wedded or unwedded, is not the only paradigm. Figures of mothers, daughters, and virgins abound; there are plenty of lascivious enchantresses, Circe's imitators. Nevertheless the unchanging symbolic framework determines that all feminine representations are based on the central position of the masculine, so that, inevitably, the roles played by female figures have their meaning in the patriarchal codes that constructed them. For men, there-fore, one can observe a whole parade of figures in which masculine subjectivity expects recognition. For women, on the other hand, one finds the selfsame parade of figures imposed by a masculine subject. But here we women find that we are the object, not the subject, of the other's thought.

The recent historical fact of female emancipation further com-plicates this picture. Since women have been admitted within the laboratories of thought (through the egalitarian principle according to which they are like men despite the fact that they are women), they are now allowed to share fully in these mythic figurations. This concession has been made, since thought is conceived of as having a universal/neutral valence (even though it has a masculine imprint), and since men's spiritual history is confused with the story of Man, understood as the human species. In this way, a female intellectual worker wishing to make a contribution to the destiny of the West is expected to recognize herself in the blueprint of Prometheus, Odysseus, and Faust, although she does not share their sexual identity. Indeed sexedness does not count at all in this supposedly universal framework that lies before her.

In all cases, what remains constant is that a woman, thought up by man in his image and un-likeness, lacks a mythic figure that can represent her as a female subjectivity capable of taking shape within her own symbolic order. Instead, she finds herself already reconfigured, and is obliged to recognize herself in the imaginary of the other. So, for women, the exercise of finding a female subjectivity in men's dreams of omnipotence through a process of adjustment and accommodation proves to be difficult and pointless. The only reward for this pointless effort is an essential image of otherness. The female subject searching for figures of her own comes face to face with stereotypes from the age-old process of deporting the feminine into the destiny of Man. It is thus inevitable that a woman will eventually insist on asking: to what extent do Prometheus or Odysseus offer me sensible images of my embodied existence as a woman? Or, to limit myself to the figures of my own sex, to what extent do Penelope's and Circe's experience match my own? To what extent do I weep with Gretchen and laugh with Zerlina?

When posed from within the field of female subjectivity, this is obviously a rhetorical question. Female subjectivity denies the patriarchal order's claim to embody symbolic figures that supposedly give meaning to the entire human species, including the functional subspecies "women." Indeed, within the scope of female thought, *sexual difference* is a fact that marks humans from the outset, since one always enters the world as either man or woman. It demands adequate representation in a symbolic order where there are two differently sexed subjects capable of autonomously adopting figures appropriate to each. This implies denying central status to the male subject in his universalizing pretensions (and hence constructing sexual difference as a role defined by the male subject). But, as a result of this demand, the masculine and feminine figures of Western culture will be thrown into disarray within their symbolic framework, with an even greater disarray in the case of the feminine figures. The rhetorical question is framed to provoke a negative answer: in the large range of samples available within the tradition, one cannot find a single figure that adequately meets the declared needs of female subjectivity. Indeed in the Western tradition female subjectivity is buried under figures of hyper-masculine men, and by figures of women constructed by men.

Nonetheless our need for mythic figures is still present. Certainly, the best solution would be for us to admit that our new thought and the fresh, new subjectivity we have constituted call for *new* figures. Literature was the first discipline to admit the entry of women as writers and to prove itself an adequate field in which to discuss their need to write, so that by now women's literature offers a significant pantheon of heroines. Unfortunately, however, I know little about literature, and even less about creating figures. So I have stolen them.

This book will deal with ancient female figures stolen from their contexts: Demeter, Penelope, Diotima, and a maidservant from Thrace. The literary context is the work of Plato. But occasionally, as is the case with both Demeter and Penelope, the context is something of a pretext, since the real and true context is the entire system of Greek philosophy and the global horizon in which it operates.

To justify this "Greek" choice of mine I have nothing to claim except my field of competence: I largely owe my interest in and familiarity with classical philosophy to the accidents of my biography. However, the specific instance does not strike me as infelicitous, since the philosophy of antiquity posits itself at the onset of our history, making its mark on the destiny of the so-called "West." In the course of the famous shift from mythos to logos, from the culture of the Great Mother to the patriarchal symbolic order that has come down to us, this philosophy accomplished an even more crucial transformation. Therefore, the classical moment of antiquity offers us the continuing presence of a transition that carries within it the fresh traces of this shift and the memory of what has been lost to patriarchal domination.

Supposedly, the documented evidence of the existence of an original matriarchy, though abundant, does not add up to the kind of proof accepted by every scholar. But here documents and proofs are not the issue. In fact, my hermeneutical project consists of investigating the traces of the original act of erasure contained in the patriarchal order, the act upon which this order was first constructed and then continued to display itself. This is how my technique of theft works: I will steal feminine figures from their context, allowing the torn-up fabric to show the knots that hold together the conceptual canvas that hides the original crime.

And theft it is indeed, in the form of a tendentious robbery that pursues its object, unconcerned with recognizing the objective quality of the figures in their context. On the contrary, these figures are freely replayed, reactivated by a new way of thinking: the categories of the philosophy of sexual difference. The theft is therefore both prejudiced and unprejudiced: it is prejudiced because it has already decided the symbolic twist it will give its object and it is unprejudiced because it does not bother to lay out any figural objectivity in the context. From this perspective it is not important to produce any documentation on the archaic culture of the Great Mother. My starting point is the feminine philosophy of our time that is founded on a maternal figure. From there we women search for, and ultimately find, the ancient figuration of the Mother surrounded by daughters and sisters.

I have already pointed out the flexibility of the figures within the play of multiple perspectives. To understand how each male interpreter managed to find precisely what he wanted, let us simply consider the hermeneutical trajectory that has reshaped the profile and pose of these figures down through the centuries. There is indeed a basic correspondence in the epistemic arrangement of these structural categories – a sort of patriarchal *basso continuo* – that holds together the fathers of the figures and those who replay them, since all of these lie within the same extended context, despite the different perspectives. In contrast, my tactic of stealing is positioned *outside* and *against* this context. It involves working with the studied naiveté of someone who patiently attempts to displace the very same language that squeezes her *inside* her own prison, without the omnipotent claim of being able to fly freely through the air. Rather, my tactic has the explicit intention to steal by leaning on theoretical axes that have already sought to dislodge themselves from their context through a radical shift in perspective.

The first of these axes is the philosophy of sexual difference. Here the revolution in perspective is of a particularly female, feminine sort. It appeals to the basic realism that comes to life when a woman observes her individual embodiment, finding that she cannot negate the sexedness which the neutral/universal noun "man" neither includes nor describes. It is not a matter of adjusting word usage. The noun "man" contains buried within it an absolute abstraction of the masculine, which is disembodied from the outset. Built on a persistent dualism of body and mind, it renders sexual difference unthinkable. Having now decided to look at herself, this woman [*donna*] finds that she is a single whole of mind and body, and demands an adequate name. This name must resonate within the kind of symbolic order where birth, the act by which embodied individuals are born and actualized, will also restore meaning to everyone, female and male. Humans always come into the world in this way, never otherwise. This is a radical revolution in perspective with respect to the existing philosophical context that began with Parmenides and has come down to our postmodern mode of thought. Here, in the new philosophical horizon of sexual difference, the basic element of philosophy is a *two*, not a *one*. Here, the original speakability of difference is inscribed as the *two*, not the *many*. And this *two* brings into language living and embodied humans, in all the splendor of their finitude.

All persons, female and male, are inevitably born from their mother's womb as finite beings. In my desire to disinvest myself from the existing context, I found the second axis of my theoretical approach in Hannah Arendt's category of *birth*. Arendt does not highlight the concept of birth as a coming from the mother's womb, but accepts the Greek meaning of birth as a coming from nothing. Despite this, the central position of birth within her work brings about a subversive shift in perspective with respect to the patriarchal tradition that has always thrived on the category of death. My tactic of stealing owes much to the perspective introduced by Arendt, which has opened up a direction where the figure of the mother can no longer remain invisible. In her work, she focuses on the site that the gaze of men has long sought to avoid for fear of staring death in the face as the yardstick of human existence. This anxiety is what gives rise to the symbolic event that constitutes the original act of matricide. It is also the basis of the obsessive desire to endure, to survive, which leads men to entrust eternal objects of thought with the task of "saving" them from the selfsame death they chose as the locus of meaning when they decided, not by chance, to call themselves *mortals* [subject to death, *morte*].

Therefore, I stole the figure of the mother first of all, snatching her from of this matricidal context. I did this already knowing that the category of birth would motivate my vision and that the category of death would entangle my context. Therefore my act of tearing apart the seams of the mother figure has laid open to view an underlying canvas so thick as to be almost perfectly capable of concealing its secrets. Yet when the needle turns in the opposite direction (of birth) this canvas is so thin that it easily unravels. I have thus given expression to a hidden intention configured as Penelope's work of weaving and unweaving. But my Penelope works on two different looms. The first composes the different figures of a feminine symbolic order. The second unties the matted threads of the fathers' tapestry. I have also given voice to the simple laughter of a maidservant from Thrace, stripping the abstract kernel of *logos* of its flesh with her realistic merriment.

Although, admittedly, my theft is both prejudiced and unprejudiced, I have not had to commit a crime against Plato's text and other neighboring texts in a completely arbitrary or willful manner. In the hermeneutical game, a measure of inherent arbitrariness has always been granted to all interpreters. Although I have frequently resorted to philological verification, I have done so not as a subtle homage to academic codes, nor simply out of professional honesty. My approach is inspired by the delight I take in unweaving the threads of these ancient texts so that the new design appears more easily on the first loom. In my act of undoing, some theoretical knots of classical philosophy have been patiently untangled. This allows the traces of a new kind of story of philosophy to unfold, revealing both its primary connective categories and its most tenacious lines of development.

I did not steal the figures from their context to let them float freely in the air. On the contrary, I stole them to relocate them suitably within the compositional canvas of a feminine symbolic order that is ready to embrace the free-flowing gestures of other female weavers. I simply wanted to choose some threads and sketch out some images. Perhaps I have sometimes insisted on giving a sense of completion to what is only a fragment. But I know that a *con-text* (a site where a text interacts with other texts) cannot be created by a single woman on her own.

As evidence of my contribution toward producing this context I can point to the largely accidental sequence of the chapters in this book. This sequence is merely intended as a way of approaching the theme of birth from multiple angles. Echoes and repetitions are inevitable, and the writing shifts in tone and register. Laborious philosophical arguments alternate with the elevated style evoked by the mythic material and with my reflections on contemporary issues. These discursive choices are imposed by the objective technical complexity of the context under examination (as is the case with Parmenides, in chapter 2), and by the topicality of the theme I have chosen (as is the case with the legislation on abortion discussed in chapter 3).

The feminine figures I have stolen have been chosen as randomly as the style in which I present them. They are related to the path along which my work has developed, rather than to a preordained plan. In fact, I knew what I was looking for, but I recognized what I found by intuitive attraction. Two figures, the Thracian maidservant and Diotima, are genuinely taken from Plato, even though within that context they play very different roles. The maidservant is a peripheral character who has only one line in Plato's text. Diotima, however, is one of the chief characters in the *Symposium*, where she delivers a long philosophical speech in which Plato's teaching can be recognized.

On the other hand, in the case of Demeter and Penelope the Platonic text is just a pretext. Demeter is merely mentioned in the etymological pun on her name in Plato's *Cratylus*, among a thousand other names. In the *Phaedo*, Penelope simply appears in a metaphor because of her work of weaving and unweaving.

Nevertheless, Plato's work is always the chief context which serves as a frame of reference for my work of theft. In my opinion, it is in Plato that the founding rite of matricide achieves its philosophical completion, even though not yet hardened into a systematic form. On the one hand, this process can be noticed in the crucial phases of the underlying logic of the metaphysics of death, rather than in a display of its definitive results. Yet, precisely because of this, the context allows conscious traces of the matricide to appear through its rips and tears.

Perhaps, as a classicist, I have the typical habit of going backwards, to the beginning, the origin, the source. In my case, this habit is intensified by the notion that the earliest philosophers are "chronologically" closer to the great matricidal felony, to what underlies the universalizing arrogance of the patriarchal order. Certainly, Plato is positioned at the start of Western philosophical history, when this initial moment is about to consolidate into a global system of metaphysics. If the real goal and the desired benefit were to "restore" a feminine symbolic order that has been effaced for millennia, then the theft of ancient feminine figures would indeed be a useless exercise. The earliest matricide is an inexorable past that is always already repeated in the language of the sons.

Indeed, it is from the here and now that we begin. My enterprise of theft is inspired by women's present needs and the categories of their current political practice. Snatched from their context, Demeter, Penelope, Diotima, and the young woman from Thrace literally stand before us, surrounded by the male code of ancient cast that has imprisoned them in its tenacious metaphysical web. The nostalgic pathos for an improbable long-lost glory will not help restore these ancient mothers to a meaningful life as female figures. They are brought back to life in the sober gestures of a thousand daughters weaving together in their mother's home.

1

Penelope

The soul of a philosophic man will reason as follows:
if it is the task of philosophy to untie the soul from the
body, then the soul itself, untied from the body, should
not return to prior pleasures and pains, nor deliver itself
to their chains, thereby doing Penelope's endless task,
as she weaves and unweaves her cloth. Rather, it should
secure protection from these, by following discourse
[logismos] and always keeping within it, by contemplating truth, the divine and what is not appearance,
and being nurtured by it. The soul thus believes that it
must live for as long as life lasts, and, when life finally
comes to an end, the soul goes towards that which is
naturally similar to it, free of any human evil.

Plato, *Phaedo* 84a–b

At her loom Penelope weaves and unravels the fabric of her cloth.
Penelope is a weaver. Her job is to weave, not to unweave. If she
unweaves, it is because she does not want to deliver herself to her
suitors. As long as she can delay her wedding to the man who
has occupied her house she does not belong to him, even though
she is under siege. Therefore she unweaves at night what she
weaves during the day, and, through this monotonous, rhythmic,
unending work, she prolongs the time of her seclusion.

For this seclusion is exactly what keeps Penelope's anomalous space open. Her space is anomalous according to the patriarchal symbolic order that sets up a particular place for her: her place as woman, and most of all as wife. But even though Penelope lives in a royal palace, by endlessly weaving and unraveling she defines her own place, where she is the wife of no one. Here Penelope is neither the wife of one of her suitors, nor of Odysseus, who has been absent for twenty years. He is elsewhere, and he has been too far away in unknown places, for too long a time to be her husband any longer, or to mark her place with his presence.

Indeed, will Odysseus ever come back? His return would (will) be the end of Penelope's unending work. In a certain sense maybe it would be the end of Penelope herself. Homer does not say (and nobody has ever asked) whether, upon Odysseus' return, she eventually finished weaving the cloth with an uninterrupted and completed rhythm, not a labor disrupted and rendered useless by undoing. This fact remains unknown and uninvestigated precisely because Penelope *is* this unending work of weaving and unweaving. Hers is a small story, repetitive and motionless, that reflects the rhythm of a single place. Her abode is always the same. It is unchanging, very far from the many diverse places of Odysseus' "great" story, very far removed from his wanderings through a multitude of experiences, his avid traveling and restless future.

Will Odysseus ever come back? Penelope's expectations grow fainter, she gets tired, her memory fades. Perhaps her spouse is dead and there is nothing left for her but to mourn him. Like the fabric of a twenty-year-old dream, Odysseus' absence is a constant, unrelenting backdrop no longer marked by the tension of expectation. This expectation belongs to a future that Penelope does not know, for Penelope knows nothing of the "great history" in which Homer narrates his stories about Odysseus. Penelope keeps herself in the present and, with her work, defines a separate place where she belongs to herself. All of Penelope fits into her small story of endless weaving and unweaving. It is her way of slowing down the tempo of a constant repetition that keeps her solitude intact and saves her from larger events. In this act of waiting, by now devoid of hope, in this major estrangement from the great Event that could put an end to the time of identical repetition, time itself, at the loom's tempo, staves off any event and renders it impossible. The dreaded wedding, like the by now improbable return of her spouse, would (will) mark the interruption of Penelope's unchanging tempo. It would break the rhythm of the loom that constitutes Penelope herself. It would end the time of a belonging-to-herself that she creates through an endless process of weaving.

For the events from which Penelope retreats with her endless work are the great events of history – the history of men, of heroes. Therefore, they are inroads onto a history that is not hers, where she will not take up a space, but only a place in an alien symbolic order. This is how things will be when Odysseus returns: Penelope will be (again) the wife of a man who reigns in his own home, finally free of enemies and assailants. Penelope will no longer have her anomalous space, her absurd tempo, the small story where she is a feminine figure preserved by Homeric memory.

Homeric memory has tried, of course, to load the figure of Penelope with quite different symbolic attributions. Imagine, for example, the faithful wife waiting for her husband, defending his place against usurpers. But the figure as such – as material for myth – has a certain malleability with respect to these interpretive intentions. Penelope has a symbolic power of her own that is open to different readings. Thus Homer's sketch disseminates clues for other possible hermeneutical trajectories. These are clues for a female symbolic order that has its own rhythms and spaces, that seeks its *figures* by stealing them from a context that has dealt with them otherwise. This theft turns a preconstituted *place* into a locus of signification where one can acknowledge perspectives denied by the previous context.

One clue that Homer's epic almost gives away to our strategy of theft is Penelope's ultimate failure to recognize her spouse. For, unlike Odysseus' dog (the faithful swineherd Eumaeus), his father Laertes, and his old nurse, Penelope does not recognize Odysseus when he arrives at the palace dressed as a beggar. She recognizes neither her spouse's face, nor the words with which he reveals himself to her. She doubts, she suspects, she demands evidence. Perhaps, then, she does not want to recognize him.[1] Or else, before the intrusion of the great event to which she will have to yield, she demonstrates that her symbolic space was not the expectation of Odysseus' return. It was her seclusion, which had by now become contented and forgetful of its cause. Indeed, when the two spouses finally recognize each other, Penelope's tale ends along with her own existence in the unique posture of doing and undoing. The great story of the wandering man ends at the same time. But it ends in a way that indicates that the story of Odysseus forms the broader setting that contains and surrounds this minor episode. Thus the brief space of the episode of mis-recognition has the symbolic beauty of a final gesture of resistance, a final holding back within the place removed from the logical order of narration. This mode of narration demands that the anomaly of the feminine figure be recontained without trace.

Still Antinous, the arrogant, threatening stranger, must have suspected that it does not take that many years to weave a cloth. Yet he knows that there is nothing he can do. The dilated time, the endless, cadenced sameness that Penelope weaves is *impenetrable*. She has no other defense or place but the dimension that comes out of her hands, and weaves her quiet time of self-belonging, taking this time from men's tempo, which is greedy for events.

Both Antinous, Penelope's suitor, and Telemachus, her son, know that Penelope's place is not the palace, but the weaving room. Though still a callow youth, Telemachus already flaunts his masculine role. He does not hesitate to send his mother to the women's quarters, among the looms and handmaids. Power and speeches are for males; for the women, the work of the loom (*Odyssey* 1. 356–9). But Penelope does not yield to her role of producing clothes at the loom, the place to which man assigns her. On the contrary, by unraveling and thereby rendering futile what little she has done, she weaves her impenetrable time. This extended intermission becomes an absolute time removed from history's events.

So by doing and undoing Penelope weaves the threads of a feminine symbolic order from proportionate materials. In this way, Homer's narrative recollection ends up rescuing from oblivion even the part it wanted to put on the record only for the purpose of making more memorable the final completion of Odysseus' story.

Indeed the great story of Odysseus opens up the time of the hero's deeds, a tempo of pressing events following one after the other. Even though they do not progress in a linear pattern, these events still mark an accumulation of "novelty" that constantly projects itself into the future and its possibile experiences. The adventure at sea, the landing on an unknown shore, become an optimal platform for the hero's *action*, the kind of action that erupts unpredictably and points the future toward one of its possible trajectories, as has been pointed out by Hannah Arendt (1959: 154ff). In the present, the action's tempo determines what is "no longer" and what is "not yet." These are reviewed in the dimension of the act that marks a breaking point and makes Odysseus famous for his stratagem. Unexpected and awesome, the wooden horse marks the end of a long war, thereby delivering Odysseus to the equally unpredictable adventures of his journey home.

The time of action, then, is characterized by the new and the unexpected. Nevertheless this action is the consummation of pressing events following one after the other. It is destined to bring on stage the things that last only a brief moment before being consigned to oblivion. For this reason, the time of action needs to preserve itself in a culture's memory so as not to disappear with the unrepeatable moment of its enactment. Homer's narration is precisely this memory. The epic is the site of its collective preservation, the legend that renders action immortal.

Obviously the time of action does not belong to the home. And it is symptomatic that it belongs not only to the mobility and infinity of the sea, but also to war and politics. These places are far from home, and the home provides a point of departure and return in relation to them. Home is a point characterized by the absence of action. Upon the hero's return, the time of action concludes with his *repose*. Indeed the symbolic universe of the Greeks delineates a time/space of toil and caring that is reserved for women (Arendt 1959: 23–45). The two spaces do not lie one "alongside" the other, but form a pattern that has Greek "Man" at its center. From this point, from the human as such in his masculine substance, women are assigned a place, a role, a time, and a function, by differentiation as a figure of inferiority and lack (Sassi 1988: 37–45). Revolving as it does around the centrality of Odysseus' voyage, Homer's narrative is emblematic on two counts: Odysseus is the champion of action, Penelope of the loom's work.

Penelope is the emblem of an order that requires her to be an industrious and faithful wife; but, precisely for this reason, she also becomes a figure who denies and disrupts the time and place assigned to her.

In the given order of things the time assigned to Penelope is predictable and productive. The queen's place is with the hand-maids in the weaving room, since the role assigned to women is that of producing garments, satisfying needs, and delivering care. This includes weaving a set of linen that will accompany Penelope in the act of remaking herself – of giving herself – as a bride. But Penelope does not weave, or, to be more specific, she undoes the weaving she has already done, thereby nullifying the role that the patriarchal symbolic order has assigned to her. Telemachus, the callow youth who acts as a frail guardian of this order, is not ashamed to send his mother away from the hall of orations and back to the weaving room. But in this room Penelope contradicts and renders vain the work of the loom, tailoring for herself an unpredictable and impenetrable time and space.

In this space shared with her complicitous handmaids, Penelope's existence is untouched by the vicissitudes of men. Her separate-ness is also different from the more predictable "woman's place," from women's function of tireless caring. This space which she carves out from day to day is home, is rootedness; it is the space where a woman stays close to herself. Here women belong to themselves completely and absolutely. Their sense of belonging comes first, and this makes other things possible.

Penelope's time cannot be touched by events, precisely because it cannot be reduced to either one of the two tempos that are alien to it: the tempo of men's actions and the tempo of wifely domestic production. Unlike the pressing intrusion of the "new" that characterizes action, this tempo, in fact, has the cadence of an infinite repetition. On the other hand, unlike the completeness of the kind of work destined for use that is characteristic of domestic production, the time marked by this cadence nullifies any usefulness or completion through its rhythmic undoing.

If measured against the action of the hero, Penelope's time is empty; if measured against standards of domestic service, it is futile. Therefore, if judgment is based on such measures or standards, this time is negative – it is a pure denial that takes place under the sign of the patriarchal order it intends to deny, implying its own dependence on that order. On the other hand, if its own measurements and standards become the basis of judgment, then this time carves out a feminine space where women belong to themselves. It displaces the patriarchal order, setting up an impenetrable distance between that order and itself.

This feminine time is impenetrable to the patriarchal order. According to masculine criteria and categories it is absurd and unpredictable. Antinous simply waits. In the weaving room something illogical is happening in the face of whose logic he can only keep away. He has to remain in that patriarchal society which the tireless industry of the loom keeps at a distance. Penelope seeks refuge neither in lack of action nor in the self-denial that comes from prolonged waiting. She weaves and unweaves, and in so doing she delineates an impenetrable space where she belongs to herself, while she prolongs the frustration of the disappointed usurpers. Penelope the queen keeps them from dominating the palace and from dominating the wife she would become if she married one of them. Thus she allows their masculine eagerness for the conquest of the throne to rule aimlessly in Ithaca.

For Penelope, Ithaca, the world, is the room of an impenetrable time where she stays with her handmaids. The affairs of state, the motives for men's actions in the world, remain foreign to her. They do not trouble Penelope's time, which neither yields nor waits. Simply to move into the world, without planting one's roots there, and with no protection for one's belonging to oneself, is a mode of being in the world that men want for women. To enter the world, that world at that time, is a way of accepting a place and role that the world of men has provided: men reserve the whole world for themselves, and assign to women a nook by the hearth. But then this nook becomes a space that is impenetrable to the motives of the world, a hearth of one's own.

The worldly time of action is kept at a distance because of its foreignness. But the time of philosophy that (male) thinkers wish to conquer is just as foreign. Their time has no beginning or end. It is devoid of hands, whose gestures can complicitously sustain the mind's desire. It is eternal.

Indeed the time of thought is solemn and immobile. It is unsullied by any bodily toil. It is the time of philosophy that was named by its own fierce and imposing father: the time of Parmenides where *being* is identical with thought. "Everlasting being" (*aei on*); the eternal that never runs out. It is devoid of gestures. No action interrupts it, not even the rhythm of Penelope's weaving and unweaving. No gesture and no body. The mind's dream reigns alone, absolute and motionless. But Penelope's time inevitably moves away from philosophers' dreams that emanate from the lofty world of ideas, where the mind's pure, unperturbed contemplation is displayed.

For Penelope's mind – almost a feminine counterpoint to her no longer expected spouse – is a *metis*, an astute kind of intelligence that understands the situation and keeps it under control. Yet, her mind does not exert control through unpredictable actions that deal with the present by pointing the future toward new occasions for *metis*. Penelope's deception is not a Trojan Horse or a cunning reply to Polyphemus. Rather, it is rooted significantly in the womanly experience of weaving, and transforms a role into its own liberating rejection.

Indeed, according to the symbolic order that assigns this role to Penelope, *all* of this feminine figure resides in her domestic work, in a sort of wholeness that does not permit a separation of body (the work of the hands) and mind (thought). Furthermore, for the patriarchal symbolic order, women do not even possess the cognitive part of the mind. The deprived portion of mind that belongs to them is quite adequate for their purposes, and is absorbed into their working body. As an inferior human animal, woman is in her domestic role a whole, made of mind and body.

So Penelope, the weaver, is supposed to be – and indeed actually is – this whole.

However, even though the entire experience inscribed in Penelope's role holds together as a whole, it is nevertheless transformed into intelligence, sustained and assisted by manual expertise. Penelope is an expert weaver. Her *metis* is all in the rhythmic doing and undoing at the loom. It cannot be separated from her body, and its object is not an eternal essence positioned outside this world, outside the weaving room where she sits with her handmaids. This *metis* does not open itself up to a time of immobile and eternal things, a lifeless time of pure thought. On the contrary, Penelope weaves a time of cadenced repetition where, day after day, *metis* is actualized in the work of her hands. *Metis* exerts control over the situation and earns the weaver her own place of signification. For in Penelope's *metis* there is no everlasting comfort from the eternal, there is rather a repetition that risks breaking its ongoing rhythm in the attention of every gesture, in the complicitous gaze of every handmaid.[2] In Dante's *Inferno*, Ulysses eventually leaves again. One more time, he leaves home to pursue "valor and knowledge" (*per seguir virtute e conoscenza*, *Inferno*, XXVI. 120). For this hero Ithaca is a place of repose, but his real element is the sea, his freedom is the unforeseen, and his valor is risk-taking. Homeless and uprooted from the present, "man" wants the future to fill the unknown where he plays out his virile essence. So the Greek hero sets sail again, and again Penelope stays at home. Waiting. But this time her waiting, if indeed she is waiting, is really purposeless, for the sea grants "man" a death that is finally appropriate to the meaning of his entire life. The hero cannot grow old and die at home, for he is precisely the "elsewhere" of an action hungry for events. The final event is sudden and far away. Let it too be swallowed up by the waves. Thus death reveals itself as the flashing moment of risk that the "new," so avidly sought after, has kept in store for him from the beginning.

Obviously, Penelope did not set sail in pursuit of her spouse. This is indeed obvious. Her place is the weaving room, not the hall where speeches are delivered nor the high seas where action occurs. In the beautiful lines of the contemporary poet Bianca Tarozzi, Penelope,

> by the shore,
> hears faraway voices in the resounding sea,
> shipwrecked sailors from long ago
> ghosts that try to seize her:
> all the wars she has neither lost
> nor won,
> all the loves she has not lived,
> the grief and the fury of heroes,
> to which she has no claim
> havoc,
> sweet screaming of the wind
> within the soul.
>
> She retraces her steps.
> For her the experience
> of the frontier
> is the raging water at the shore –
> for Odysseus the crash,
> and a dreadful death
> against the rocks, into legend.
>
> (Tarozzi 1989: 21)

Thus for Penelope the seashore is a limit. It is her experience of the frontier. Conceptually this limit is not symmetrical with the limit experienced by Odysseus. In fact, his limit means death, the end of a sequence of unpredictable actions that delineate his story. Nevertheless this is the end that delivers him to legend, and renders him immortal in epic memory, precisely by turning his life into a memorable story.

Indeed, in Greek the concept of death is configured as limit and measure. In other words, in Greek, death is *the* sign of human finitude, where every other finitude is comprehended and evaluated. This is an unbearable sign, a door that opens onto nothingness, in the face of which epic memory can offer some solace. In a more decisive way, solace can also be found in the kind of pure thought that male philosophers describe. In this sense, for Odysseus the sea is a place that has always held the extreme

limit, even long before Dante wrote his canto on the death of
this Greek hero. Indeed the risk of death is always present at sea,
in this unreliable liquid element that washes unknown shores. The
voracious waves present a risk. And the sea becomes a route
toward, and a setting for (mindless) scenes of death: Polyphemus,
Circe, the Sirens. Shipwrecks, routes, points of arrival, traversing
a "newness" that offers itself over and over as an occasion of
death. Thus Odysseus experiences the limit many times before
yielding to it permanently, almost as the trajectory and destination
of his characteristic wandering. He is tested repeatedly before
succumbing to the last test. But the unpredictable culminates in
a dreadful scene in which nothingness finally bursts open; a
nothingness that is always lying in ambush and therefore constantly offers a threshold to the last unpredictable event. Death
defines *its* dominion in the wars, the sorrows, and the fury of
heroes. It is always present insofar as it is always challenged, functioning as a measure of the challenger's excellence. In the Homeric
world of mortals, only legend can win over finitude and save
humans for eternity, but only the challenge of this finitude can
become legend.

Not so for Penelope. The dominion of death defines her
home – her island – as a region foreign to both "the wars that she
has neither lost nor won," and "events" having nothing to do with
her about which she does not know. For her, the extreme limit
of experience is neither the entirety of the sea nor the irresistible
ambush of death, but only "the raging water at the shore," a daily
sight that dissolves its dreadful matter into innocuous ripples.
Certainly, if the patriarchal order becomes interpretation, it
imposes its finitude on Penelope. But if interpretation could see
with Penelope's eyes, this finitude would become a confinement
where the self-belonging she has won carves out a proportionate
space around her.

Just as her wifely role was disavowed in the process of weaving
and unweaving, and thus became the place of impenetrable
separateness, in the same way the seashore now becomes the
extreme limit of Penelope's space, not as a prison, but as something that excludes an alien world inhabited by men.

Penelope knows that the sea belongs to Odysseus, and she

allows him to measure his deeds and story on the yardstick of death. She allows the legend to recount wars, sorrows, and fury. She allows the Greek hero to turn his back on his birthplace – Ithaca, his home, his room, his mother. He no longer seeks a sense of roots, his abode there, nor the quiet finitude of one born from the maternal womb. She allows him to test the sense of his own being in the power of death.

Penelope knows that she is not like Odysseus, and does not want to be like him. (Heroines in armor, not Amazons, but soldiers among soldiers, will populate the epic imagination of future poets!) Nor does Penelope yield to the role, the confinement that Odysseus imposed on her. With her room she makes her own legend. By now the suitors are defeated and Odysseus is gone forever. Even her arrogant little son is no doubt at sea. I see her laughing with her handmaids, together in a group, weaving garments to suit their needs, and telling of how they kept the suitors at bay, of how they discovered the joy of being with each other, working and thinking together. I see her. I see her, in that amazing island that now separates two estranged worlds with a mythical clarity. She speaks of birth and rootedness, rather than death and adventure. I see her looking out from the windows at the edge of the raging water that separates her and her handmaids from the heroes' deeds, and allows them to stand on their own ground where their gestures weave an initial space for a kind of feminine freedom that will no longer be threatened. This first horizon of belonging leaves masculine industry elsewhere, in the realm of death that it has chosen as its measure, and as the farthest point on its blood-soaked horizons.

We women will have to leave Penelope's Ithaca. But precisely because Penelope was able to stop there, we will be able to leave a *place* without forgetting or losing it.

In order to speak about Penelope, I have chosen an epigraph from Plato's *Phaedo*, not Homer. To be honest, in Plato's text on the immortality of the soul, Penelope makes only a fleeting appearance. Her function is metaphorical. Plato's thesis is this: by leading one's thinking toward eternal objects suitable to pure thought (pure ideas), philosophy *unties* the soul from the mortal body. Therefore those who lament the fact of death, which is the definitive untying of the soul from the body, are bad philosophers. Exactly like Penelope, they retie (or wish to keep tied) what they have already untied with philosophy, in an endless labor that fails to progress in a single direction, and therefore renders futile whatever work has been done.

This metaphor is strange, to say the least, founded as it is on a logical inversion. For (good) philosophers, the absurd, the negative, consists in reweaving what they have unwoven. This is the case at least in the patriarchal perspective that Plato shares with Homer. For Penelope, obviously, the absurd consists in the opposite, in undoing what she has done. Nevertheless, something very interesting happens precisely in this inversion. If in Plato's metaphorical word play Penelope's weaving appears to be an act of retying the soul to the body, then one can see that Penelope turns the task of philosophy upside down. The metaphor is therefore worthy of further investigation. But this should not be done without a careful analysis of the Platonic context in which it appears.[3] The *Phaedo* takes place in jail, a short time before Socrates drinks the hemlock that delivers him to death. Death is thus the theme and setting of Socrates' last speech; a death that is feared and mourned not by Socrates himself, but by the male friends gathered around him. He welcomes death as a good thing, like the definitive untying of the soul from the body which allows the soul to return to its original abode, close to the "things that have always been" to which the soul is similar by nature. Therefore, for the philosopher, as for Penelope, there is a *home*, an abode which is immobile, unlike the seafaring mobility of the hero. But unlike the weaving room, his abode is not on this earth. It is the kind of home that serves to distance him and uproot him from the earthly life into which humans are born.

Indeed, death is nothing but the *untying* of the soul from the body that leads the soul back to its original home. It is a definitive untying, and for this reason it is perfect. Nevertheless, the philosopher can experience it also during his lifetime, but only in an imperfect, temporary form. In life, the agent of this untying is (pure) thought: the thinking part of the soul (*nous*) which can pull itself away from the body through philosophical exercise and

attain the contemplation of "the things that have always been."
The dichotomy between the living world and the world of ideas
thus becomes the canvas and backdrop of Plato's argument.

Through this form of reasoning the complete entity that constitutes each human person thus splits in two: the body, which
belongs to the living world, and the soul, identified with the
activity of thinking, which belongs to the world of ideas. The
separation of body and soul is structural: they have different
origins (the first is biological and material, so to speak, the
second, metaphysical and divine). So it could be said that the
individual living person consists of a temporary union of these two
parts, a stitching together of two elements that lasts until the
definitive untying of death.

The mythical image of this tying together is the *descent* of the
soul into the body which takes place at the time of birth. But here
birth is a *fall*, a negative event. This immediately turns the place
of origin from which each person actually enters the world into
a simple (and devalued) place of appearance "on earth." This
place causes what is eternal, or what will eventually return to
eternity, to languish along with mortal matter. Aside from
mythical representations that use the image of metempsychosis,
Platonic teaching is indeed quite explicit in assigning the substance
of human nature, virtue (*arete*) to the noetic soul. The soul
experiences its sojourn in the body as an imprisonment. It feels
pulled down toward transient matter that distracts thought from
its abode near pure ideas (the things that are eternal).

The ties of the flesh, the chains of pleasure and pain, the
rhythms of the body and the passions of the heart tend to keep
the noetic soul down here, in the living world, unless the soul
becomes capable of untying itself from the body to contemplate
pure ideas through philosophical exercise, thus anticipating the
complete untying that comes from death, in an act of untying
which is "unfortunately" not definitive.

What emerges is the persistent "living for death" that constitutes
one of the most consistent principles in the philosophical tradition
of the West. This is not the first time that such a principle has
been formulated, since Plato's doctrine is a sort of re-elaboration
of Orphism. But certainly this principle emerges here in a complete

and well-argued way, and within a philosophical doctrine that will exert enormous influence on tradition. Not coincidentally, Hannah Arendt takes her distance from this tradition and plants the roots of her thought in the category of birth. In her view, the otherwise rather strange historical reality of an ancient mind–body dichotomy, with its strong hostility to the body, persists along the entire history of Western philosophy (Arendt 1977: 1. 163–4). First in line is Plato, who observes in the *Phaedo* that "the philosopher appears to be pursuing death to those who do not study philosophy" (*Phaedo* 64b).

Those who do not study philosophy and do not experience thinking as a distraction of the mind from the world, a turning toward the "things that have always been," are therefore correct in grasping the authentic intention of philosophers: the pursuit of death, the perfect untying of the soul from the body. Plato is keenly aware of the similarity between the goal of philosophy and what those who do not study philosophy think of philosophers. The later tradition, however, up to and including Heidegger, ignores the similarity between the two perspectives, failing to grasp that the "secret" that philosophers "live for death" actually corresponds to most people's opinion of philosophers.

To be fair, a philosopher who lives for death like Plato's Socrates entrusts himself to a doctrine that has already removed death from the dimension of life, since it has turned life – understood as the eternal life of the soul – into an abstract concept, untouched by birth, life's journey, and its end. Indeed what we are witnessing here is a semantic shift that separates the concept of life from the concepts of birth and death, which, nevertheless, belong intrinsically together in the experience of every single living person. This is made possible because the life of the soul, an eternal life without birth, change, or death, functions as a paradigm. Thus life, defined on the basis of the eternal life of the soul, loses its connotation of birth and death, leaving these within the bodily dimension. We have thus two meanings for the word life: the *true* life of the soul, and the *mere* life of the body that moves, grows, and changes between birth and death. The individual living human, a union of body and soul, contains both, but s/he has his/her center and destiny in the true life of the soul.

Much more than mere life, true life harbors the divine life of the eternal in a temporary prison suspended between birth and death.

In this doctrine the intersection and the semantic displacement of life and death are quite complex. But these are fully played out in the separateness of body and soul and in the identification of the soul itself with its noetic part, namely thought, its best and most substantial activity. It is worth the effort to disentangle and analyze this complexity. At this point Western philosophy has already celebrated its glorious triumph over matter. By trivializing the necessary bodily dimension of living, it now inhibits the symbolic translation of sexual difference. In other words, a separated and dematerialized embodiedness can more easily conceal its sexual connotation, always marked by difference. Hence the male gender can easily claim to be neutral and universal.

Indeed the opposition between soul (*psyche*) and body (*soma*) is explicitly thematized in the *Phaedo*. These two parts of the living human person stay together for as long as the human person lives out his/her earthly life. But they separate with death. In death only the body dies, while the soul returns to "the things that have always been" to which it is akin. Therefore the mortal body is a prison for the soul, which by its nature is akin to the "things that have always been." It unties itself from this prison precisely at the moment of death, a moment that therefore also restores the true life of the soul.

The semantic displacement of the concept of life is therefore crucial. In fact, strictly speaking, the body itself does not even possess a living dimension (even though it has an earthly life), for this dimension comes at birth with the *descent* of the soul into the body. The soul is therefore not only the locus of eternal life, but also the principle of earthly life. Life on earth originates precisely when, by falling into the body, the soul *ties itself* to it, and ends when the soul *releases itself* from it, with the death of the body. Like an external burden, the body weighs upon life. Nevertheless, strictly speaking, this body does not possess life. It appears that birth belongs to the body only in negative form, as the act of "supplying" the soul with imprisoning and transient matter which comes from the mother's body. The act of death, on the contrary, belongs to the body in a fuller sense, for death is an event in which the body is the only protagonist, though for the soul's benefit. Death constitutes a beneficial act, the definitive release that the soul can experience in advance through the excercise of philosophy.

This separation implies devaluing the body to mere accident. Plato emphasizes this by attributing to the body the well-known connotations of jail and prison. In contrast with the Judeo-Christian tradition, the separation of mind and body is evident chiefly in the doctrine of metempsychosis. Indeed this theory, which is narrated in the myth of Er at the end of the *Republic*, assigns individuality to the soul but not to the body, so that every soul descends into different bodies in its various reincarnations. To be fair, at this point it is no longer even possible to speak of "individuality" in the strict sense (or, in any case, in a modern sense), for every soul is characterized by a specific tendency that often brings it to choose a reincarnation that suits it, rather than by an individual identity. For example, we read about a soul that had been previously incarnated in Tamiri the singer and now chooses the life, and thus the body, of a nightingale. We also read that Atlanta chooses the life of a male athlete (*Republic* 620a–c). What makes the myth interesting here is not just how the complex symbolic mechanism of metempsychosis is explained; rather, it is the emphasis that is placed on the insignificance of the body with respect to the soul. The significance of the body is so slight that it might belong either to an animal or to a human, or, within the human species, either to the female or to the male gender. In other words, the separation of mind and body is total, and the body is a burden that the soul chooses for some of its specific qualities (voice, agility, etc.), indifferent to species or gender.

The body from which the philosophical soul unties itself either through the exercise of thought or, finally, through death, is indeed a minor thing. Insignificant, accidental, and always an embarrassing dead weight. Still, this weight cannot be ignored. So much so that thought must continuously be on the alert, must work relentlessly at untying, since the body, until claimed by death, always lies in ambush claiming as its own the soul and mind it incarnates. Furthermore, death itself can be the occasion of a final distortion, though certainly not for Socrates, who welcomes this definitive untying as a good thing, but perhaps for his companions, who weep over the final untying of Socrates' soul from its earthly prison and, like Penelope, would like to retie what philosophy has released by turning this exercise into a continuous and contradictory doing and undoing. On the contrary, the work of the philosopher proceeds only in one direction, and Socrates testifies to this by dying of his own accord. It unties, it releases, it undoes the corporeal ties that bind the soul. And it does not reweave the fabric of soul and body that keeps thought at a distance from its home.

As I have anticipated, Plato's metaphorical use of Penelope's work, and more precisely the logical inversion that it encapsulates, contain some interesting symbolic elements in relation to this discussion. Socrates accuses the companions who cry over his imminent death of imitating Penelope in weaving back together the soul and the body which philosophy had allowed them to untie. The metaphor is macroscopically imperfect in its juxtaposition of Penelope's work with the hesitations of imperfect philosophers. Her work has a rhythmic cadence, and is thoroughly sustained by a precise intention that gives it a certain inexorability in following through with its two operations. In the philosophers' tying and untying there is neither design nor *metis*, only accidental and uncontrolled contradiction. But this is not quite the point yet.

Plato's metaphorical word play concentrates on Penelope *as a weaver*. Given that the philosopher is not talking about woolen yarn but about the soul and the body, the scandal is not that Penelope undoes what she has done, but that she reweaves what she has already unwoven.

But has she? It is the word (*logos*) that educates the soul to recognize its true nature. And it is the true discourse of philosophy that accomplishes the act of undoing bodily ties, thereby opening up to thought the experience of its heavenly abode. But, like other women, Penelope does not belong in the hall where speeches are made. Her place is in the weaving room. Therefore, if untying is the work of philosophy, Penelope does not untie, she does not unravel. She simply weaves together what the philosophers have undone.

Besides, the speeches of the *Phaedo*, and more precisely the philosophical discourses that untie the soul from the body, take place in the cell where Socrates is sitting with his male friends during the final hours before his death. Xanthippe, his wife, has been hastily thrown out. This is not a place for women. Socrates does not want any women in the cell when he comes close to accomplishing that "living for death" announced by philosophy. Thus while waiting for the perfect, definitive untying, he attains the experience of death through a final dialogue about his own death. Women are unaware of the untying of the body in which true philosophy consists. They scream and yell in the face of death. Exactly like bad philosophers.

But not quite. For by crying, bad philosophers reweave what they had (rightly) unwoven. But women are unaware of philosophical discourse because they are excluded from it. For women this tie is essential and now seems to dissolve for the first and last time. But perhaps not quite. For Xanthippe Socrates simply dies; he is no more. She knows nothing of the split between soul and body, and simply stays within the experience of her individual life where mind and body are joined indissolubly together.

And so Penelope the weaver, like Xanthippe, truly weaves together what others, not she, have undone with philosophy. In this manner, the metaphor functions precisely because of its strange logical inversion: the untying of the soul from the body (a positive operation) belongs to philosophy and the discourses of men; the tying of both together (a negative operation) belongs to women. This is why Penelope, famous for her extraordinary act of unweaving, turns into an emblem of the opposite act. She weaves together soul and body, she reties the threads of a thick fabric where embodiedness is knotted to the soul, and most of all to thought, the part of the soul that (male) philosophers wish to untie from the body more than anything else. Penelope tangles and holds together what philosophy wants to separate. She brings back the act of thinking to a life marked by birth and death. She intertwines and holds together the elements of the living world, the only real world, allowing the philosophers to persist in their desire to inhabit the world above. This eternal world knows neither birth nor death, only an infinite duration of pure thought.

Penelope is indeed a weaver. In Homer's epic she is mentioned for unweaving what she had already woven. But she did this to define her time and space, and to snatch them from the events that tried to draw her back into a symbolic order not of her own making. She is a weaver. And now perhaps, thanks to Plato, we know what she continued to weave with her handmaids: after the event of Odysseus' death at sea she quietly went on in the experience of finitude delineated by her self-belonging. She continued to weave the individual whole made up of body and mind that had already appeared in her *metis*: the reality where to live is most of all to be born and then, only at the end, also to die. The interweaving of intelligence and the senses is where all humans exist as part of their gender, not as eternal souls fallen into a body like many others bodies, regardless of species or sex. A woman like her handmaids, Penelope holds their intertwined thoughts and bodies in a home of their own, leaving elsewhere the masculine exercise of death.

Death claims many rituals for its kingdom: Odysseus' heroism, which is measured on risk, and Socrates' knowledge, which finds accomplishment in death. Both are cases of a "living for death" where death itself is the emblematic figure of a kind of finitude defeated and eternalized at the same time, by the legend that grants immortality, and by philosophy that dwells near the eternal.

But in the weaving room, these women neither separate their philosophy from the body to grant it eternal duration nor entrust their experience of finitude to death in an arrogant desire for immortality. The world of ideas and the sea are not theirs. Having let men go forth to their adventures at sea, they stay together quietly, exchanging looks and words rooted in the individual wholeness of their existence, now so evidently gendered in the feminine that this life shared in a common horizon allows every woman to recognize herself in another woman.

They are weaving and laughing in their quiet abode.

2

The Maidservant from Thrace

> While looking up at the sky and scrutinizing the stars, Thales fell into a well.[1] Then a quick and graceful maidservant from Thrace laughed and told him that he was far too eager to find out about everything in the heavens, while the things around him, at his feet, were hidden from his eyes.
>
> Plato, *Theaetetus* 174a

A young female slave whose name remains unknown to us laughed at Thales, the earliest philosopher in history.

Though only a minor female character in Plato's vast and distinguished repertoire, this Thracian maidservant found a way to avoid oblivion, even if the memory that tradition has retained of her has little to do with the genuine truth hidden in her laugh. Yet this truth is still accessible, if snatched from the text and stolen from its context. For subsequent tradition has in fact reduced the maidservant to an anecdote that is supposed to illustrate the inability of simple-minded people to understand philosophical speculation.

Plato's anecdote has been taken up repeatedly by different writers down through the ages, sometimes with radical changes and variations, to signify the contemplative attitude of the philosopher, misunderstood and mocked by the common people. In this way, the laughter of the maidservant, later pluralized by Socrates as "the laughter of the Thracian servants" (*Theaetetus* 174c), becomes paradigmatic of the simple-minded obtuseness of ignorant people in relation to theory (*theoria*), which is to say in relation to the contemplation of truth enacted by thought. Truth is a "higher reality" that supposedly distracts or pulls thought (or the thinker) away from the ordinary things of the world. The thinker becomes so distracted that he stumbles and makes a fool of himself in the ordinary affairs of the world, where he is absent-minded and out of place. According to Aristophanes' plays, a philosopher lives in the clouds. This figure is still with us in the popular image of the absent-minded intellectual, clumsy in the practical matters of everyday life since he has more elevated things to think about.

Indeed, what the anecdote shows most clearly is this very distraction, this being pulled away. A kind of distraction, so to speak, that is intrinsically visible from two different perspectives: that of the Thracian maidservant who laughs at the philosopher, and that of the philosopher himself who pays no heed to her derision, holding *theory* as a higher value than the world of ordinary experience from which theory distracts or pulls him away. In the age-old tradition of Plato's anecdote this dual perspective has been utilized with contrasting meanings, according to the needs of different circumstances and authors. One finds a valorization of the mocking position when the user of the anecdote wishes to take an anti-metaphysical position, given that metaphysics, for the very fact of being *meta ta physika* (beyond physics), suits contemplators of the heavens who do not pay attention to the things of this world. The valorization of Thales' position (or Plato's) comes to the fore instead whenever a writer wishes to underscore the ignorance of those who mock philosophy, failing to understand the importance of speculation and the contrasting banality of common sense.

As I previously mentioned, in the course of time the anecdote has been retold by different authors with some significant modifications, obviously aimed at the "moral" that is to be drawn from it. Hans Blumenberg recently published a study of its long hermeneutical history (Blumenberg 1987). One can readily observe in reading his well-documented work that the element that undergoes the most radical modifications in Plato's anecdote is precisely the figure of the maidservant. She is transformed into a nasty old woman by writers who want to underscore the obtuseness of those who despise philosophy, and she is replaced by an Egyptian wise man when Thales' position is belittled in anti-metaphysical terms. Plato's misogyny, softened by a mention of the girl's pleasing appearance, is thus polarized in the historical development of philosophy. The maidservant becomes an old woman (having lost her physical attractiveness) when a negative role is assigned to her, and she turns into a man (a sage) when a positive role is called for.

There is, however, a specific passage in Blumenberg's study that is particularly significant in this regard, even though it does not contain an explicit expression of misogyny. It is interesting for the way in which the author demonstrates the *invisibility* of the female sex as a locus of autonomous signification, which is the premise of every possible form of misogyny. In fact, Blumenberg himself declares the sex of the maidservant in the original Platonic version of the anecdote to be inconsequential and unimportant (Blumenberg 1987: 21). What is especially significant for him is the fact that the character who mocks Thales, regardless of gender, is a slave and comes from Thrace. A slave, because uncouth and ignorant in the extreme. Of Thracian birth, because Thrace evokes "the depths of a world ruled by strange gods: *female*, nocturnal, primeval gods" (Blumenberg 1987: 21).

But if this is how things are even from the perspective of a modern, skeptical consciousness intent on interpreting Plato's ancient anecdote with meticulous scholarship, the Thracian servant really laughed from her heart, and with good reason.

She laughed with the laugh of a woman whom Plato saw as young and attractive, and whose image he therefore endowed with the trait of attractiveness, a trait that is assigned to women as their special "value." A physically appealing female figure is thus juxtaposed in symbolic polarity with the masculine wisdom of the true philosopher.

Plato in fact inserts the anecdote into a long discourse where Socrates describes the true philosopher. Here the philosopher focuses his attention on investigating the nature of the "things that are," meaning pure ideas, and is completely indifferent to the "things that are near him" (*Theaetetus* 174a). So, like Thales, he becomes awkward or clumsy when he has to deal with the things around him, provoking the laughter and mockery "not only of the Thracian maidservant but of all others present" (*Theaetetus* 174c). Such people are obviously ignorant, limited to the superficial experience of the senses, and incapable of rising to the heights of pure thought.

But Thales, philosopher *par excellence*, was indeed able to rise to such heights. Plato's anecdote has him watching the stars. Thales is said to have been an expert on the affairs of the heavens, capable of predicting eclipses and foretelling the seasonal harvests. He looks up, way above the world full of things that wither and die, and contemplates the eternal, regular movement of the stars, where everything is constantly repeated according to the unshakable necessity of the laws of the heavens. Rapt in thought, his mind in a state of contemplative calm, Thales is distracted, pulled away, from the earthly world of everyday life. Besides, the transient things of this world *are* not really what they *seem*. Though differing from each other in their multiform, changing semblance, all things are water, Thales declares in his famous precept. Their principle is wetness; a principle of *one* that makes things into a *whole*. A principle that is "deeper" than the "superficial" manifestation of things, deeper than the way these things might seem to mere sensory experience. Like the regular motions of the stars, they are "higher up," visible to everyone's eyes but governed by an eternal law that only the mind can discern and understand, thus gaining a lesson on the nature of what is true.

In this way, a sense of a world that is elsewhere, that is not of this world, begins to emerge with Thales, the earliest philosopher. This "elsewhere" is declared a higher and more profound place, and these qualities still denote in ordinary language what is true and better, in contrast with what is base and superficial. Thus, right from the outset, Thales steers philosophy in the "right" direction.[2] Up above, one finds the regular movements of the stars which know neither birth nor death but exist forever, and down below, a multitude of transient, individual experiences and evanescent forms. These are passing manifestations of a deeper principle. They are appearances caught between birth and death, toiling to sustain the brief life of a dissolving moment. The meaning of these mere appearances lies elsewhere, and is accessible to those capable of transcending appearances without being misled by the deception of the surface of things. Their being is real, precisely because it lies elsewhere.

Two worlds are thus set forth. One is apparent, and the other real. Plato's language is already capable of distinguishing them with ease: the world of the Thracian servant, made of the things that "lie close at hand" (below), and the world of philosophy, made of the "things that are" (which exist up above, in the depths of the heavens). The crux of Plato's distinction lies in the claim that the realm of the "things that are" is real and true, while the world of the things "close at hand" is devalued as merely superficial *appearance*, pertaining to the deceptive experience of the senses. This distinction has brought about the philosophically tenacious dualism between being and appearance.[3] More importantly, it has turned our sense of reality upside down, so that the world of the living becomes the phenomenal shell of a kind of truth that is removed from the realm of the senses and is accessible only to thought.

The term *reality* is itself an effect of this dualistic schism. "Reality" has no close equivalent in the Greek language. Based on the Latin word *res*, the term has eventually come to mean the same as the Greek *ta onta*, the *being* of the "things that are," which is precisely the name that Plato gives to pure ideas.

The philosophical shift that occurred between Thales and Plato gave increasing emphasis to the split between being and appearance. It further reduced the significance of appearance to mere *semblance*, namely, to unreliable deception. By contrast, this enabled being to assume the characteristics of an eternal and unchanging duration, which eventually came to coincide with the activity of pure thought. In this shift the equation of being with reality functions as a progressive negation of the reality of the living world (a dematerialization), which deprives the things that are close at hand of their meaning, and even of their existence, as is witnessed in the writings of Parmenides.

The only hint of resistance (or derision) in the face of philosophy's negation of reality is to be found in the maidservant's laughter. Her laughter provides a hint of precocious intelligence, since she already observed while watching Thales the earliest, decisive moment of this philosophical tendency. But her laughter also indicates an almost prophetic intelligence. In fact, between Thales and Plato came Parmenides, the great annihilator of the world of life, now sacrificed to the realm of being. Certainly, compared to the unrelenting momentum of philosophy's development, the maidservant's laugh may seem a very small thing indeed. But it has the merit of condensing in a moment pregnant with truth the boring futility of argumentation. The maidservant's argument is strong with the power of facts, with the power of one who belongs to this world where she has her roots and lives out her individual existence. She exists above all in a female existence, which has no locus of signification in the celestial sphere of philosophy.

The water drawn from the well, the care of bodily needs, and the preparation of nourishment constitute the maidservant's locus of existence. While absorbed in the contemplation of things that are higher up, Thales does not even see the well. Later Parmenides, who is preoccupied with the kind of being that is one and unchanging, denies the very existence of wells.

Parmenides, precisely. In his writings the split between being and appearance, between the realm of thought and the world of life, becomes so deep that appearance and the world itself risk disappearing, risk being annihilated without trace. At this point, only the pleasant laughter of the Thracian servant can accompany us in our analysis like a promised relief, as we struggle toward a reading that is crucial, though wearying.

In the proem to his work (*Fragments* B1. 1–33), Parmenides reverently describes a withdrawal from the world that has an aspect of ritual initiation. Young girls, the daughters of the Sun, accompany him in a chariot drawn by trained horses. Thus accompanied, he passes beyond the gates of Day and Night and is greeted by a goddess who shows him the path of truth, namely, the path where "being is and cannot not-be, while not-being is not and must not be" (*Fragments* B2. 3–5).

All of Parmenides' writings, or at least all the fragments that have come down to us, are dedicated to clarifying the basic precept of the goddess. But the proem does not introduce this precept superfluously. In fact, it clarifies at least two points. Parmenides, a man, becomes wiser by detaching himself from the world of mortals. In this withdrawal he is assisted by women. The daughters of the Sun as well as the goddess who instructs him are female (and even the horses are specified as mares). Both points merit a brief discussion.

This detachment from the world has a decisive effect, not only for Parmenides but for the entire history of Western philosophy. In fact, the higher realm to which Thales directs his thoughts is represented here explicitly as the realm of truth, the locus of pure thought. The world, inhabited by *appearances*, is discarded as false and unreliable. It is even described as the deceptive shadow of nothingness. In other words, what we find here is the most radical formulation of the schism between abstract thought and the direct experience of the world that has been inherited by philosophical tradition. The word "abstract" should not sound excessively modern here. It is supposed to indicate precisely a kind of detachment through which thought decides that it can stand on its own, carving out an expanse of immobile eternity that is then presented as the standard of a higher truth. This truth is supposedly up above, and it even runs counter to the evidence of people's everyday experience. Similarly, the term "direct experience" should not sound too naive: it is supposed to indicate a perception of the world actuated by the organs of perception, and above all by sight which registers the way in which the world manifests itself through appearances in movement. Obviously the mind, inextricably rooted in the wholeness that constitutes a living person, is immediately involved in receiving these manifestations. In contrast, according to Parmenides, the noetic faculty of the human mind becomes isolated and detached, and sensory experience is left behind.

The realm of pure thought thus becomes the *abode* of the thinker who forgets that the world of appearances precedes whatever region the philosopher can *choose* as his own "true" abode, where nonetheless he was not born (Arendt 1978: 92–3). In effect the philosopher abandons the world of his own birth in order to establish his abode in pure thought, thus carrying out a symbolic matricide in the erasure of his *birth*.[4] This act of matricide extends to everyone, insofar as all humans are born of woman into a world of appearances, a world where they, too, "appear" as they come forth from their mother.

Humans are thus split into thought and body, truth and life, and the second term of the dichotomy is allowed to slide toward insignificance. The split sets up a trajectory that explicitly establishes philosophy's tendency to disavow reality. Soon the concept of man (*anthropos*)[5] – named in the masculine singular but with a universal-neutral valence that is supposed to indicate humankind as a whole – will make its way into philosophical language. From there it will move into the everyday language that we still speak. Immediately, man named in this way will indicate that his substance, the authentic foundation of his being, lies in his ability to think. "Man is a rational animal," Aristotle's famous definition proclaims. Bodies, feelings, and the deceptive senses supposedly belong elsewhere. At times, these are a troublesome burden, while at other times they provide clues to something that must be verified by thought. Yet they are always the clumsy, unreliable baggage that those incapable of investigating their true basis entrust to appearances. The realm of surfaces cannot perceive height or depth. Nor indeed can it perceive truth, which, unlike facts, is never tangible or superficial.

On this route toward the de-realization of the world, we find women bringing and leading Parmenides on high. Obviously, the tradition of the Homeric invocation "Sing, O goddess!" comes into play here. We must not forget that Athena, goddess of wisdom, is a woman. Nevertheless it is astounding that female figures inaugurate the route toward abstract thought, where philosophy celebrates its patriarchal glory. In fact, within the symbolic order of philosophy, women are either completely absent, or they appear as naive and ignorant persons just like our Thracian maidservant, or function as divine female mentors like Parmenides' goddess and Plato's Diotima. Thus we find a subtle and ambiguous symbolic game. It almost seems as though women (excluded from the realm of thought both in reality and because of the "unthinkability" of their gender) become the sacrificial food for the journey toward the realm of philosophy that will exclude them. In other words, it almost seems as though philosophy was attempting to leave a residual trace of the matricide committed at the outset. In any case, it is a female figure who opens the route to the paternal realm of metaphysics, where pure thought no longer holds any (living) root. Thus, the maidservant's laughter is an anomaly. As such, it constitutes a clear indication of women's alienation from the kind of knowledge that has excluded them, and in the service of which they ultimately offer to act as dutiful facilitators.

In fact, with Parmenides something definitive happens to philosophy and to the history of philosophy. *Being* is named as the locus of truth. Even Hegel would concede that no other term is as weak, empty, and indeterminate (Hegel 1969: 78).[6] Yet philosophy has made *being* its realm.

Obviously, this is also a question of language. To make things clearer, an agreement must be reached about what is meant by the term *being*. Typically, philosophical textbooks propose an explanation according to which the ancients claimed that each thing – whether this or that particular thing – first and foremost *is*, and finds its foundation in *being* for this very reason. Thus, following a line of argument that is not completely persuasive, everything is, and *being* is the principle (*arche*) that permeates and substantiates all things.

What we have here is an "existential" understanding of the term "being" which indicates that each and every thing is, exists, is present. Yet things are not that simple. In fact, the Greeks inextricably mixed together the "existential" and "predicative" valence of the verb to be (*einai*). For example, in the expressions "honey is" and "honey is sweet," the "is" confuses and merges its meaning as "existence" with its grammatical function as a linking verb. Some modern interpreters consider famous texts such as Parmenides' *Fragments* and Plato's *Parmenides* as examples of the ancients' confusion on this subject.

Indeed, things are not so simple. The "confusion" has in fact marked the language of philosophy and inscribed itself in tradition as a metaphysical legacy, eventually evolving into other forms. Yet it has never been abandoned (in spite of intentions to the contrary). Hence something more than a crude mistake in syntactical logic must be involved here.

And in fact there is something else at work, given that the juxtaposition between *being* and *appearing*, the active kernel that confines truth to the realm of being, has left its mark on thousands of years of Western culture. It still influences the epistemic structures of the so-called sciences of our own day.

With Parmenides, the philosophy of being makes its brash, decisive entrance into the history of thought. It achieves this in a drastic way, claiming that only *being* is – one, all, compact, and complete – while *not-being* is not at all. Not-being is nothing, and is therefore unthinkable and unspeakable. It is completely banned from true speech, which can say only *is*, and can never say *is not*, since, as the goddess states, "it is neither speakable nor thinkable, given that it is not" (*Fragments* B8. 8–9). The main problem with Parmenides' philosophy is not the drastic claim that brings to the fore the elementary juxtaposition of *being* and *not-being*. Even the least brilliant student in a typically unsophisticated way will immediately agree that what is *is* and what is not *is not*. A more serious problem is to be found in the consequences that Parmenides draws from such a simple doctrine. Here we see a much more shocking juxtaposition of the realm of being with the entire world that everyone experiences from day to day. According to Parmenides, this world, or the experience of this world, belongs to the realm of not-being, and hence does not exist at all. The world thus falls under the rubric of the *unspeakable* and the unthinkable that keeps *not-being* outside discourse. This is where we can perceive the shocking strangeness of Eleatic teaching: since movement and multiplicity imply *not-being*, they have no reality or speakability whatsoever. They are not. They merely float as deceptive *appearances* before the sightless eyes and deadened minds of those who do not know the true realm of being (*Fragments* B6).

Thus Parmenides' initial juxtaposition hardens into a dichotomy of more serious import. On one side – the side of truth –

there is *being*, which always is and never is not, which is one, eternal, immobile, and compact. On the other side – the side of appearance – there is the world in its multiplicity and mutability, inhabited by *not-being* and hence prey to unspeakable nothingness.

In interpreting Parmenides it is crucial to grasp the way in which not-being is identified with the world. This is the root of the negation of multiplicity and movement that already shocked the ancients. It is also the root of the juxtaposition between *being* and *appearing* that Parmenides passed down to tradition. In fact, this "appearing" has the negative meaning of "seeming," of illusory perception, of what is untrue and does not exist at all. And what we must now especially investigate is the omnivorous potential of *not-being* with respect to the world which has been relegated to the deceptive realm of appearance.

The world is a plurality of many things that differ from each other. They differ, and therefore each one is different, each one *is not* the other. But things also change, since change is first and foremost the prerogative of the living. Thus each thing in the course of time *is not* yet or *is not* any longer the same. *It becomes*. In terms that have by now become classic, philosophical terminology describes what can be experienced as a multiple "becoming manifest." This *becoming* of all things (through birth, change, and death) is expressed in terms of *not-being*. To put it another way, multiplicity, of necessity, implies difference and alterity, and in Greek difference and alterity are terms of *not-being*: not being the other, not being yet, not being any more.

It is precisely the lexical valence of *not-being* that allows Parmenides to "deduce" the nullification of the world from the affirmation that *not-being* simply cannot be, and to declare this as a truth readily shared by others. Even though this affirmation posits both *not-being* and the-*being*-that-always-is in their abstract form, it nevertheless falsely claims that arriving at the truth in this way is an effective method of banning the mention of *not-being* from discourse in all the forms and modes it can occur. In its lethal linguistic power Parmenides' *not-being* leads the manifest qualities of the world of life toward annihilation. Multiplicity, movement, change, and transformation can be experienced and perceived first and foremost by the senses. But they are merely apparent, precisely for this reason.

Here, in fact, the moment when pure thought reserves for itself the pronouncement of truth is also the moment that heralds and institutes the drastic distinction between the source of thought and the source of sensory experience. Thought has abandoned this source in order to soar upward in unsullied purity. The proposition "being is and not-being is not" is constructed by pure logic. It is then assumed as a true principle from which consequences can be consistently drawn. It hardly matters if these consequences lead to a denial of the evidence of sensory experience. In fact, if the logic of pure, disembodied thought is *the* criterion of truth, whatever conflicts with this logic can only be false, which is to say "apparent," only in the sense of "seeming" or unworthy of belief.

One can thus begin to problematize the unsophisticated student's reading of Parmenides' principle. "Being is and not-being is not" is a proposition constructed according to a way of thinking that separates itself from the wholeness of human experience, and, in this self-ordained separateness, offers itself as the locus and criterion of truth. In the words of Parmenides, *"to be and to think are the same thing"* (*Fragments* B3), so that whatever does not fit into the realm of uncontaminated thought is of necessity untrue. It is apparent, illusory, and without any credibility, since it can be witnessed in the course of the day-to-day experience of everyone. In other words, what we have here is an unconditional abstraction that claims to be the only reality. From its own standpoint, it judges the world as unreal, in spite of the testimony of ordinary experience, simply because the world can be inscribed in the realm of not-being that thought has identified with nothingness, and hence with the *unthinkable*.

But the world and *not-being* (which encompasses the world in the language ordained by the logic of pure thought) collapse into nothingness. Along with them, appearance (*doxa*) begins to assume the traits that Greek philosophy has handed down to tradition: the traits of a "becoming" in which things either are or are not. In other words, they appear (*dokein*) according to the constitutive mutability inscribed in the term appearing, which is always a "not-being yet" or a "not-being any more" what something or someone is. This is above all a continuous changing that disempowers and consumes what is becoming, up to the definitive point of not-being that is death itself.

The realm of true and solid knowledge (*episteme*) is deployed in opposition to appearance, *doxa*. This realm of knowledge is taken up with the kind of thought capable of contemplating the "things that always are," as Plato emblematically defines pure ideas, a realm that is in any case inhabited by external and disembodied essences.

What is important is that this dichotomous Parmenidean structure has been preserved by philosophical tradition, despite the fact that philosophy itself (as far back as Plato) was quick to reintroduce *not-being* into the realm of the *episteme*, which is to say, the true discourse of which philosophy properly consists. This occurs precisely at the time of Plato's well-known "parricide" of his mentor Parmenides, through which the younger philosopher reinscribes *not-being* in the category of the *different*. In Plato, the different becomes one of the major types of thought, thus rendering multiplicity thinkable.[7] Nonetheless, the reappropriation of not-being does not impinge on the dualistic structure that cuts off the locus of truth from the world of life, the eternal from the ephemeral, thought from the body, the universal from the contingent, science from mere appearance. In other words, the transformation of the Parmenidean concept of *not-being* which absolutely is not into the Platonic notion of the *different* simply enables the naming of the manifest qualities of the world. Yet it does not prevent their reality – their place of signification – from lying elsewhere, and precisely in the realm of thought that considers sensory experience and everyday lives a burden and an obstacle. So the disavowal of the world's reality in the name of Parmenides' not-being continues to exert its power, and appears to be a theoretical kernel that contains something more profound than a logical problem, something more tenacious than a question of dialectics.

At this point the question could be formulated as follows: what precisely is there to be found in Parmenides' absolute negation of *not-being*? Or, what is it that lurks within *not-being* that must of necessity be nothing, at the cost of losing the world itself to mere illusion?

It is death that causes so much fear, as it lurks ominously at the center of not-being. Nevertheless, "not-being" is never absolute not-being or nothingness, since it offers multiplicity, difference, and mutability. It is instead a sign inscribed in the world presented to the experience of living, sentient beings. This is a world of "becoming." The world "becomes," in the sense that everything changes and is no longer the same, and yet it does not continue this process of becoming for all eternity, in a kind of perpetual transformation, but ceases at the moment of death. Here, in death, becoming reveals that changing was rather a dissolving. In other words, nothingness, into which *what is* finally disappears, manifests itself as the destination of becoming, and at the same time as its substance. To put it yet another way, what *is*, over time, "is not" any longer the same. This transformation carries inscribed within it the definitive *not-being* that is the ultimate destiny of what is.

Thus the focus on death consigns the meaning of becoming to an image of dissolution. According to Melissus, one of the Eleatic philosophers, "if things were to change only by a hair's breadth over a period of ten thousand years, in the course of the ages they would be completely destroyed" (*Fragments* B7. 2). Therefore, far from possessing a positive meaning within the realm of experience, change and transformation (which are ultimately the concrete sign of life itself) quickly become a sorrowful foreshadowing of death. For death is nothingness, a nothingness into which everything capable of becoming (living and changing) disappears. This actually shows that *becoming* is merely the transformation of being into nothing: a concept that humans cannot tolerate.[8]

The terrible concept that causes such anxiety is intolerable only for those who at least accept the existence of death, those who do not insist on denying that death occurs under one's very eyes, and sooner or later befalls everyone. There is already a distortion in perspective in this way of measuring the entire sense of becoming against the standard of death. This distortion is deeply entrenched in the Greek tradition. One has only to think of the Homeric tension between the human world of *mortals* and the other world of immortal gods. And yet it is in the teaching of Parmenides that the melancholy sense of becoming, its identification with what is destined to decay, reaches its conceptual fullness. In fact, in this doctrine, becoming is fully committed to the figure of nothingness. At the same time nothing, taken up and judged in the sphere of pure thought, is rendered unthinkable, inconsistent, untrue. Thus transported into the realm of pure thought, only to be evoked, judged, and expelled from there, nothingness is now despoiled of all sense of reality and hides its terrifying power in the figure of death. Nothingness is indeed nothingness: it *is not*, and because thought and being are identified with each other, it is therefore unthinkable, unpronounceable, unspeakable. In short, it is not real, since thought alone, which is identified with being, determines the true standard of reality. Thus, to say that nothingness is devoid of reality is to disavow the reality of death. This disavowal logically brings with it the becoming that has assumed the category of death as its intrinsic destination and measure.

In other words, if death must not be, then likewise the world must disappear. According to this logic, death, the emblematic image of nothingness, has no being, and hence does not have to be experienced; nor does the world which carries in its bosom the fleeting, mortal presence, the changing, transforming movement of multiple individual elements in the process of becoming. It hardly matters that death and the world have a claim on reality insofar as they are available to and are experienced by everyone. This experience has been excised by pure thought and declared as illusory as its objects. It belongs to the treacherous and fluctuating realm of appearance that philosophical truth annihilates as the empty shadow of a dream, or, more specifically, a nightmare that the sage has shaken off by entrusting himself to his obsession with infinite duration.

It is indeed symptomatic that Parmenides' philosophy evokes a dichotomous framework where death and the world of appearances conceived as nothingness lie on one side, while on the other side we find being and thought which are identified with each other in an infinite duration. This duration not only lacks death, it also lacks birth, since we have gone far beyond the immortal valence of the Homeric gods who were somehow born at a certain point in time. Here we are in the presence of the eternal which is not born and does not die, but always is. Thus the central importance of death begins to reveal its unexpected consequences, as the conceptual standard of not-being. With consistent logic, this centrality swallows up birth in the annihilation of nothingness. Here birth means *not-being* yet, a kind of coming from that nothingness that supposedly does not even exist.

We can thus observe the emergence within philosophical discourse of a kind of monotonous refrain whose obviousness lies solely in the power of repetition, and not in the power of facts. Death and birth are named together as a couple in a sort of specular polarity, exactly like the "not being yet" and "not being any longer" that the law of philosophy declares absurd and unpronounceable, insofar as they belong to the not-being that absolutely does not exist.

Indeed birth and death belong to being, which is identical to thought and alone is true.

> Dike concedes neither birth nor decay,
> so to be born is absurd and to die unbelievable,
> without beginning or end, since birth and death
> are pushed far away in the name of persuasive truth.
> (*Fragments* B8. 13–14, 21, and 22–3)

Birth and death are thus related to each other in perfect symmetry as a coming from and a returning to nothingness. This may indeed be the most obvious indication of the centrality of death that permeates the painful representation of the human realm, already marked by the nothingness of death at the very moment of birth.

It is hardly by accident that in Greek humans are called *brotoi* (those subject to death), in accordance with an older tradition that Parmenides accepted and affirmed. The allusion to death in the naming of humans is thus logically inscribed in a context where birth is unproblematically categorized as the symmetrical opposite of death. This has been carried down in philosophical tradition as a tirelessly repeated platitude that has never been investigated.

I will return later to the disavowal of reality implied in this obsession (at which the Thracian servant had good reason to laugh). For the moment I want to emphasize how philological investigation reveals the hardly casual use of the term *brotoi* in the writings of Parmenides. In fact, Parmenides also uses the term *anthropoi* to indicate "Men" (*Fragments* B1. 27). But he uses it at the outset, when the goddess reveals the doctrine of being. *Brotoi*, in contrast, is used later to indicate those who do not know how to rise to the truth of philosophy and thus wander, blind, deaf, and confused, through the false world of appearances. Therefore, people who live in a world where death is mistakenly considered real are truly *mortal*, truly transient, and subject to death. In their world each person is eventually destined not to be any more, and mortality is something real which has meaning. It is conceivable, expressible, thinkable, and yet completely impossible according to the doctrine of "truth."

Inhabiting the realm of pure thought (which renders the human thinker no longer mortal but eternal), the doctrine of truth knows nothing about bodies, or about the dead. Thus, inevitably, it does not even recognize birth, which is rooted for all humans in the maternal body. The young Thracian servant may very well laugh. She is accustomed to seeing the swollen bellies of pregnant mothers touched with gentle, knowing gestures by women who encounter others like them. How can she call all of this a coming from nothingness that absolutely does not exist?

We know that the rigidity and absoluteness of Parmenides' teaching does not hold up for long. It may well be said that death is unbelievable and that the world is non-existent (in its multiplicity, movement, and so on). Yet even to Plato, this remedy for anxiety in the face of human transience seems really excessive. Not, as one might think, because it is an impractical one (given that people die just the same, and it seems foolish to call this fact a troubling illusion), but because philosophy itself runs the risk of getting stuck in the pure and simple repetition of being one, unchanging, eternal, and complete. As Plato himself declared, he wants to *save phenomena*. He wants to explain the sensory manifestation of the things of this world as the particular, changing multiplicity of something that nonetheless has its roots elsewhere, precisely in the realm of intelligible being, the realm of pure ideas. "The things that are" are always eternal, without birth or death, and are yet different from each other. In fact, each idea (the idea of the well, the idea of man, the idea of beauty, for example) *is not* the other. So here not-being is restored to the realm of true knowledge under the guise of *the different*. Philosophical discourse can thus continue its infinite articulations without being locked any longer into the monotonous repetition of being. In this way, with Plato, multiplicity, or difference, returns to the intelligible realm of being as the problem of *the one* and *the many*. This realm preserves the blueprint of the uncontaminated and eternal existence of its objects (its thoughts), while elsewhere, "farther down" beneath the heavens, lies a world of particular, transient, contingent things where no truth whatever can reside.

And it is indeed symptomatic that, despite Plato's important adjustments, the dichotomy constructed upon Parmenides' negation of not-being survives as a constant framework within philosophy. Eventually philosophy moved beyond this drastic pre-Platonic doctrine that went so far as to proclaim unthinkable the concepts of the multiple and the changing. But the dualistic framework founded on Parmenides' teaching still persists. What is kept is precisely the distinction between *episteme* and *doxa*, mind and body, the world of ideas and the world of life. Even though the world of life is no longer regarded as nothingness, it is still the site of mutable things. These have their ontological foundation in pure ideas (the object of *episteme*), namely the root and sense of *being*, of which mutable things are merely the contingent appearance. Insofar as s/he is body, matter, phenomenon, each human person participates in the sadness of the mutable world. But insofar as s/he is endowed with the capacity for thought, s/he also belongs to the world of ideas where the transiency of all mutable things "is redeemed."

The centrality of death, which attributed the trait of eternity to objects of thought, has nevertheless had a decisive influence on this dichotomous dualism. Though no longer absolutely negated as nothingness, with no reality whatsoever, death itself remains as an affliction of bodies alone, the sad and temporary prison of an intellectual soul that has its home in the eternal realm. In other words, Plato holds that death belongs to human experience, but only to the bodily part. Humans do not properly consist of this part, but they drag it with them like a heavy and troublesome burden. As such, death no longer means the disappearance of humans into nothingness, but the nothingness of a body that constitutes a heavy encumbrance. As such, death is tolerable, even liberating, because it is merely physical. As such it inscribes itself perfectly into the dichotomy between the reality of the eternal and the frailty of illusory appearance, a dichotomy founded and produced by the centrality of the concept of death.

Death actually releases from the body the thought that Penelope's gesture keeps tied to it, in her desire to achieve a human existence whose measure is a sense of individual wholeness.

Thus for Plato the algebraic sum calculated by pure thought does amount to zero, as was the case with Parmenides. The world continues to appear, and with the world, death. But this is not a constitutive appearance of the world's being, contained by an experience destined to embrace it. Rather, it is merely an illusory seeming grasped by the deceptive senses. It is grasped by a physical sensibility that has been cut off from thought, for this sensibility too is phenomenal, apparent, always poised on the edge of nothingness.

The calculation does not quite work out at zero, since the world and the body hold out. Their resistance is nonetheless considered mere illusion, the crude empiricism of ignorant people who limit themselves to facts, and do not look for the meaning and foundation of these facts in the separate realm of pure thought. At times they even mock pure thought, just like the Thracian maidservant on a starlit night.

Indeed it is hardly an accident that the one who laughs at philosophy is a humble slave girl. But it is also emblematic that philosophy enlists female figures as its self-destructive propitiators. Certainly, it would be easy to say that the maidservant's gender is irrelevant, that she is simply a symbolic allusion to the ignorance and foreign origin of slavery, as Blumenberg has claimed and tradition confirmed. In short, the figure of the Thracian servant is supposed to indicate people "of little importance." And she is still less important since she is also a woman. But the symbol has free play in its allusions, and the female gender of the servant, removed from the biases of its context, can be placed at the center, with the focus on its mark. In this way it can be stolen from a tradition that considers it unimportant, or simply interprets it as an indication of benign misogyny. For this figure definitely contains some misogyny, however embellished by Plato. Yet therein also lies a feminine truth that the Platonic text carries within it *despite* its intentions: like some type of feminine word that the text itself conveys while failing to comprehend it, a small news item that is simply reported, its meaning never investigated.

I am not sure that she was a servant or that she came from Thrace, but some woman laughed at the philosophers. A quick smile can often be seen on the faces of women as they observe the self-absorption of brainy intellectual men. Philosophers have put this down to biased ignorance, not realizing that it is the expression of a kind of detachment that locates the roots and meaning of female existence elsewhere.

The Thracian servant really laughed because she fully belonged to the world of life. She belonged to it not only as a slave, accustomed to giving service by drawing water from the well, but as a woman marked from the beginning by sexual difference, before being marked either as slave or free person. This woman is unrepresented in the sphere of being to which the philosopher devotes himself. The philosopher (truly ridiculously) calls this woman "man."

In fact Socrates, Plato's Socrates, proceeded in the company of Parmenides on Thales' heaven-bound path, going far beyond the stars. For Plato's Socrates, the locus of truth is found in the ideas attained by thought. It is in the heavens, where a splendid and divine testimony of what is unchanging, ordered, and eternal remains. These ideas constitute precisely the "things that are": the idea of beauty, justice, and equality, but also the idea of the weaving shuttle and the well. The idea of man.

Man, as in the Greek singular noun *anthropos*.

Inevitably, the negating process of philosophy soon produces its linguistic effects. In Plato in fact we find the consolidation of a philosophical terminology that names in the singular the idea in whose *being* (one, eternal, and undivided) the plural phenomena that pertain to it are categorized. A multiplicity of beautiful things find their reality and meaning in the idea of the beautiful (the beautiful in itself, the beautiful itself), a multiplicity of just actions in the idea of what is just, a multiplicity of wells in the idea of the well, and so forth. But with the idea of man, something very peculiar occurs, since it categorizes women as well as men. It is true that in the word "man" the masculine has a neutral–universal valence, which is exceptional in its capacity to indicate the male gender as well as the entire human species, and this was already evident in the customary use of the plural "men." But the adoption of the Greek singular *anthropos* puts greater emphasis on the abstracting effect or the "dematerialization" carried out in this linguistic operation.

The Thracian servant laughed during the period when philosophical language was being consolidated (Snell 1960: 227–45). The philosopher cares so little about worldly things that he stumbles while attending to them. In fact, according to Socrates, the philosopher must investigate "what man is, and what is proper for man's nature to do and suffer, as distinct from the nature of other things" (*Theaetetus* 174b). The response to this investigation is well known: the intimate nature of man is the intellectual part of his soul, with which he is capable of knowing pure ideas (not least of which is the idea of himself). With this reply, popularized in the famous Aristotelian formula "man is a rational animal," the negation of reality magically comes full circle. Always immutable and elsewhere from the living world, the real being of man coincides with his atemporal contemplation of "the things that are."

What causes the Thracian maidservant to laugh is already fully contained in Socrates' question, even though the formula claiming that man is a rational animal makes it even clearer. What the philosopher investigates is indeed man. Such an extraordinarily polyvalent and ambiguous essence denotes the male sex, though the word has a neutral–universal valence. In the world of life, the

Thracian servant, who is herself first and foremost a woman and a living person, encounters individual humans gendered male or female. But with respect to this world, the philosopher presumes man himself as real and true, a general representation that abstracts from individuality and apparently from gender. This "apparently" symbolizes the most deceptive strategy through which the disavowal of reality is put into effect. The servant is a woman, she is gendered in the feminine, but her being woman is considered appearance – mere embodiment – since her being, true or false, lies in the idea of man. Thus this woman who has her being in the idea of man is logically a man, assigned by chance to a female body.

Even for Thales, who *is* a man, male sexual difference pertains to the world of appearance, except that for Thales the male gender is elevated and affirmed as the idea of man. This idea universalizes male sexual difference as the sole gender of humans' real true *being*. In short, on its tenacious trajectory of logical abstraction, philosophical language first named women and men with the plural word "men," and then shifted from this plural term to the singular "man." By that time, the idea of man had lost all its specificity, and was thus devitalized, inhabiting the eternal realm of being. In this way philosophy hides the fact that men in their irreducible plurality – not Man's essence – inhabit this earth. It also hides the visible fact that both men and women live in this earthly abode (Arendt 1959: 9).

In fact such poor, contradictory logic (from which none of the modern languages has yet freed itself) produces tenaciously dangerous effects of disavowal, of de-realization. In the idea of man who always immutably is, what is lost and devalued as mere appearance is the individuality of living humans. But what is especially hidden is female sexual difference. Reduced to empirical specificity, this difference is a fortuitous embodiment *which falls outside* the dimension of ideas and their signifying power. This specificity nevertheless disempowers, and thus renders inferior the essence of the human signified in the idea of man. In fact, if the essence of man is indeed pure thought, or so-called rationality, a "man" to whom a female body befalls – namely, a woman – immediately sees this fortuitous embodiment translated into a disempowerment of her own rationality. In fact, through the bodily difference that marks her, a woman is a deficient human person, a man who is less-than-man. This (il)logical operation unduly separates the body from thought. On the one hand, it holds the body as accidental and, at best, unimportant. On the other it translates the body into the disempowerment of intellectual power if the body is gendered female.

In this way the strange case of the neutral–universal valence attributed to the masculine term "man" reveals its true basis. In the idea of "man" it is precisely the human male that is referred to, a male universalized to stand for the human species as a whole, and women are thus categorized as one of his inferior specifications. Women do not constitute the "other sex" of the human species, but rather a subspecies (*Ipazia* 1988: 3–5).

Thus for Socrates the Thracian servant, like any other woman, has her real, true being (though disempowered and inferior) in the idea of man. There is indeed a very good reason for the maidservant to laugh.

She is a mere servant, not a goddess, not the daughter of the sun, not a priestess. And she laughs. "Servant" is a possible polite translation of the Greek term for slave. It is not a bad translation. Servant means belonging to the everyday world, familiar with the services and concrete rhythms of life that the patriarchal order assigns to women. Women's confinement to the "sphere of human necessities" completely serves the masculine sphere of thought. The care of indispensable and needy bodies is indeed entrusted to the domestic realm. The servant, as a female figure of oppression, is nonetheless capable of a desecrating laughter. Her laughter resonates within her confinement to the "sphere of necessities," where it appears more real and concrete than the ceremonial aura of the propitiating female divinities imagined by Parmenides.

Indeed in the teaching of Parmenides the goddess leads the philosopher into the realm of pure thought in order to celebrate the glories of the patriarchal order. In this realm neither bodies nor even the world exist, and birth is described in a masculine way as a coming from nothing rather than a coming from the mother. Though limited to a role that the patriarchal order ascribes to her, the Thracian servant demonstrates with her laughter an unrestrained freedom. She also demonstrates the concrete fact that this world, just as it is, limits all men and women. Just as Penelope renders her subordinate role futile with the infinite cadence of her gestures at the loom, similarly, the even humbler role of the Thracian slave girl does not prevent her from having a certain feminine realism.[9] Feminine realism is anchored in facts, restoring to facts the meaning they demand in a brief moment of laughter. These facts exist in a world that "resists" every intellectual effort to erase it.

The servant is destined to daily toil. Her tired gesture seems to provide an exhaustive symbolic transposition of her destiny. But here it becomes the image of its eminently theoretical operation. This act of intelligence cuts itself off precisely from the everyday gestures of work. In a moment of revealing laughter, it illuminates the entire illusory substance of Western thought. Thus although the young Thracian woman is a slave, she is not a pathetic figure, she does not represent the passive docility of female oppression. She is a figure bursting with laughter, and her laughter serves as a frame for a few incisive words of wisdom. The things of the world are hidden from philosophical thought, where Thales begins the process of de-realization, of disavowing the reality of the world.

So her confinement to a woman's role (so much harder for the slave girl) can be understood as an essential distance. This distance is not simply produced by woman's assigned place within the male order. Rather, it comes from its own roots in female experience, an experience that stays away from the claims to truth put forward by the male order. Indeed the Thracian servant is excluded from philosophical knowledge first and foremost as a woman, and only secondarily as a slave. She realizes that within the male order of knowledge she *really is not*, since there is no woman in the idea of man. The idea of man is said to be neutral and universal, without gender, be it masculine or feminine. If this is the case, in the world she holds onto as her truth, the Thracian servant does not know of any human born of woman who is not perceptibly, factually, and incontrovertibly male or female. Thus the young maidservant stands in the world of life which she holds as real and true. The male order calls this life appearance and its own abstraction reality, but the maidservant keeps her distance from that mode of thinking. Her distance is produced first by concrete essence and then by choice or exclusion.

She stands by the truth, keeping her distance from the false truth of what appears to be true.[10] And she is laughing, not merely at the ludicrous accident that happens to the man who tumbles into the well because he thinks of the well as mere appearance and not reality.

She is also laughing at something quite different. She is laughing at the foundational falsehood that the language of the West inherited from philosophy. Here the concept of verisimilitude (that which simulates the true) is generated from the dematerialization of what constitutes truth. This disavowal of reality penetrates everything, takes root, grows, and covers things up. Thus the world of life does not disappear but lies hidden. It is a forgotten presence that continues to seek signification in a true language that might encompass the basic experience of living within its own horizon. The world of life would no longer be considered the blind and meaningless realm of the empirical, the fallacious counterpart of the language of true ideas. For humans, the fact of life is always individual and gendered, even though it is hidden by an abstract language that names man as neutral and universal. This *fact* is indeed basic. Life is always gendered, never otherwise. This remains true and is renewed at every birth, but its persistent concealment can render life hidden from abstract language, even though it cannot eliminate its presence.

Facts get in the way of philosophy, and philosophers know it. This is evident when philosophy makes an effort to deprecate the realm of the *empirical*, reducing it to the deceptive shell of a deeper, more elevated truth, a truth that is hidden according to the established dichotomy between being and appearing. In this way, the strategy of concealment is compounded and ultimately conceals itself. Indeed the truth at which theory looks (supposedly hidden by facts) is revealed to be a sort of verisimilitude. Theory defines facts as mere deceptive appearance, and consequently verisimilitude hides these facts and keeps them buried. In this way, the verisimilitude that philosophy feeds on conceals the truth of facts, despite Heraclitus's claim that it is philosophy that "likes to hide itself."

These facts are as hard as the well hidden from Thales' philosophical thoughts. Though hidden from Thales, the well does not disappear. Rather, it swallows up the unfortunate thinker in an absolutely concrete way. Nor do even more important facts disappear, like the fact that humans come into the world engendered in difference. We come into the world as we are born from our mothers. This coming into the world has birth, not death, as its standard and measure. Death does not make any distinction, and women and men die individually just the same, even though men have claimed for themselves heroic death on the battlefield as a platform for their valor. And, later, with the kind of intellectual heroism that befits such thinking, philosophers have pushed death itself into the insignificant realm of bodily events.

The ancient female laughter of the maidservant is thus a sign that can be snatched from a context that considers it a mark of ignorance. This laughter itself becomes the figure of a female symbolic order that has the power to expose a philosophical discourse whose mendacious structure renders it liable to outrageous lapses. This conceptual structure collapses heavily in the face of the ready laughter that shatters its seams with resounding mirth. Thus Thales' tumble in the well and the servant's laughter are coupled like a unique and ancient factual truth, so much more genuine since there is no malicious satisfaction in the servant's words, uttered with convincing gravity: "The things around you, at your very feet, are hidden from your sight."

If it had not been for that ancient laughter that still resonates with a female voice, these facts would have been hidden for a long time, without scandal or protest, through the efforts of an order of verisimiliutde founded on death. The philosophy of the eternal has tried to suppress the sense of life, by relegating it to the unbearable anguish of a becoming haunted by nothingness. It is this sense of life that the female voice redeems, in a tone of liberating laughter.

3

Demeter

It appears that Demeter was named after the gift of
food she gave (*didousa*) as a mother (*meter*).

Plato, *Cratylus* 404b

Demeter, the mother, the Great Mother. The name Demeter is one
of the words used by the ancient Greeks to indicate the Great
Mother. Many cultures present the figure of Demeter in their
philosophy of origins. In these cultures the figure of the Great
Mother indicates "an absolute deity; since she is the only one
to show evidence of possessing the secret of life and fertility, she
has the power to transmit this secret at her discretion to human
beings, to the earth, and to plants and animals" (Giani Gallino
1989: 8).

In Plato's pun on the words giving (*didousa*) and mother
(*meter*), then, this original meaning has already been lost. Here
the mother is a nurturing creature: she gives food and with it
she cares for and protects life. However, she is neither the source
of life nor the repository of a secret passed on to the whole living
cosmos "at her discretion." There is little doubt that Plato's
wordplay – as the whole *Cratylus* confirms – is a way to play

with etymology, often just a mockery of the ancient philologists. But the pun is inscribed consistently in the patriarchal symbolic order that has established itself precisely on the erasure of the symbolic order of the Great Mother.[1] This paternal order reigned unchallenged in the age of Plato, and claimed masculine deities as its own symbolic figures of rule-givers. It is symptomatic that death replaced birth as the fundamental paradigm of this order.

Indeed the masculine figure at the center of the myth of Demeter is the god Hades, lord of the underworld or kingdom of the dead, located under the surface of the earth. But this complex myth has a basic, rather simple structural level. Above, in the warm light, is the mother. She represents the act of regeneration and birth. Underneath, in the shadowy cold, is death. Hence, birth and death, the feminine and the masculine kingdoms, function as oppositional categories. Most importantly, they function as categories that give rise to a conflict which is apparently resolved by a mediation marked as "agricultural": the seed goes under the ground to be reborn in the warm season. It journeys from dark to light, from winter's death to spring's birth. But as always happens, the myth is also complex and cannot be reduced to a mere symbology of seasonal cycles. A trace of conflict or, more specifically, of encroachment can also be read in this myth. The agricultural symbology is superimposed on this conflict as an external artifice. It does not contribute to mediating and resolving the conflict. To put it another way, the *context* of the myth contains archaic symbolic elements together with their own transference/erasure onto a different figural arrangement. While this arrangement changes the sign of these archaic elements, it neither succeeds in resolving the symbolic conflicts they represent, nor does it manage to streamline them in a linear, unidirectional narration. In this way the context speaks of a symbolic order of the Great Mother, defeated and effaced by a patriarchal society that twists its original meaning, but leaves clues of this distortion in the context, thereby providing evidence of the crime.

According to Luce Irigaray's interpretation in *Sexes and Genealogies* (1993b: 131) the myth of Demeter speaks precisely of an interruption in a feminine genealogy, violently overpowered by the patriarchal order. This order is oblivious to birth and emphasizes death. Having separated philosophy from embodiedness, being from appearance, it has turned this dichotomy into the philosophical system of all systems, and the "destiny" of the West. The myth tells of how Demeter's daughter Kore is abducted from her mother by deception, and thereupon is taken to the underworld to be wedded to Hades, ruler of that kingdom. Demeter becomes desperate. While her daughter is away she no longer generates, rendering the whole earth *sterile*. The threat of sterility is a threat to the existence of humankind and the world, persuading Hades to send Kore back to her mother for a period of time every year. This is the warm season, during which fertility returns to the earth. In the cold season, which marks the departure of the daughter from the mother and her descent once more to the underworld, the earth turns cold and sterile again.

Indeed, the central theme of the myth, apart from its agricultural interpretation, is the power of the mother, which is inscribed in all of nature as the power both to generate and not to generate. This is an absolute power that presides over the place from which humans come into the world and over nothingness, as birth-no-more, the endpoint of the maternal continuum which also marks symbolically the end of the world.

In this respect maternity is the matrix of the arrival of humans into the world. Their arrival is rooted in nature, or *physis*. The Greek word *physis*, from *phyein*, to be born, connotes the act of generating as a way of manifesting oneself, of growing, and of becoming present. Indeed, according to Aristotle, the first two meanings of the word *physis* are: "generating things that are born" and "the primary material element from which the thing that is generated proceeds" (*Metaphysics* 1014b). And similarly in Latin the word *natura* derives from *nasci*, to be generated, to be born, to grow (Arendt 1959: 131). So the stem of the word "nature" indicates that to arrive into the world (and to encounter the world) is to be born. This being born is obviously always gendered, at least in the eyes of those capable of looking at the fact of birth in a realistic way.

Indeed universal "Man" is never born and never lives. Instead, individual persons are born and live their lives gendered in

difference as either man or woman. But every human born, male
or female, is always born of a woman, who was born of a woman,
who, in turn, was born of another woman, and so on, in an
endless backward movement toward our origins. This maternal
continuum delineates the feminine root of every human being. A
living person is merely a single instance of human generation,
sexually differentiated within a natural order that generates by
gendering (Irigaray 1993a: 108). Therefore humans carry sexual
difference inscribed within them, as the how and where of their
coming into the world, of their appearance and arrival into the
world.

As a consequence there is no nothingness before or beyond
physis. *Physis* is simply the world's boundless mode of being. It
is preserved for men and for women by the mother. Until Hades'
act of abduction breaks and upsets the order of birth – namely for
as long as the daughter stays near the mother – the maternal
power of both generating and not generating remains unknown.
At least it is not recognized for its capacity to bring the process
of regeneration to a complete standstill, as results from Demeter's
decision in the myth. In the order of birth, nothingness has no
place. Maternal power extends itself between two sequences of
infinity: the infinity of a maternal *continuum* that lies in the
past of every human born, male or female; and the infinity of
a maternal *continuum* that presents itself as a future possibility
when a woman generates a daughter. Both infinities, past and
future, origin and perpetuation, always exist through the feminine.
This feminine is not an abstract form: it is a portion of infinity
that humans can sustain, and where each discrete individual takes
root and finds meaning.

In the myth it is precisely the mother who stops generating
when the daughter is snatched out of her sight. This act brings
nothingness onto the stage as "birth-no-more." Nature reacts to
injury by coming to a standstill. Consequently the maternal power
to generate is coextensive with the reciprocal visibility of mother
and daughter. It is not enough for Demeter to know, to ascertain,
that Kore is elsewhere, married to Hades. She wants to *see* her
daughter, to be seen by her, and to welcome Kore within her sight.
Phyein becomes possible only in this reciprocal visibility (Irigaray

1993b: 132). When *visbility* is denied, *phyein* stops. It is no longer a manifestation of regeneration but the foreshadowing of a sudden end.

This is the end of the world, precisely because the world is *physis*, neither confined nor preceded by nothingness. Indeed the world bears nothingness within its heart, in the possibility of stopping the process of regeneration inherent in maternal power. This immense power contains its own absolute negation: "no longer" becomes *nothingness*, a nothingness that is not beyond this world. It is not the nothingness of male philosopers who identify it with death which provides the measure the world, and its destiny; it is rather the *nothingness* of birth, a mute petrification of *phyein*: the desolate land where even death dies of unmourned immobility. Far from being a "coming from nothing," birth is a coming from a mother. Demeter presides over the nothingness inscribed within her maternal power as the very possibility that constitutes her being. The force that constitutes her power is presented as an absolute paradigm, since the silencing of the entire *physis* is a traumatic response to the violation of an original maternal order.

In the original situation, which presents the reciprocal gaze of mother and daughter, the mother has in fact already generated. Accordingly, all of nature exudes birthing, the "nascence" implied in its name. The power of maternity is free in this cosmic order: the power of not regenerating does not yet know the "nevermore." This power is not the threat of nothingness. It is a quiet secret of birth entrusted to woman. Actually, here Demeter does not represent a continous and rhythmically uninterrupted birthing. Rather, she represents the link between human birth from woman and the gendered regeneration of everything in nature. Demeter has a daughter; she was born of her and is of the same sex. In the natural/natal order this is sufficient for everything to continue regenerating in various forms. This is because the human infinity from which we come entrusts the possibility of its future to a feminine genealogy in which it is rooted. In fact Demeter does not *have to* generate. Rather, it is because Demeter generated a daughter, whom she kept close to her, that all of nature continues to flourish in its own rhythms.

Nevertheless, the natural/natal order of gazes requires that mother and daughter be visible to each other. It demands that we look at the female gender in relationships between mothers and children. Every woman belongs to this gender, and finds in this gaze the measure of her own appearance and being in the world. Hence we have a feminine stem in the meaning of *theorein*, the "gaze" that the male philosopher directs toward the eternal. This *theorein* does not look up; it does not divert its attention from the earth. It is a *theorein* that extends horizontally in relationships of correspondence, in the direction of birth and the arrival of humans into the world. In fact, the world that appears to this gaze and within this gaze is marked by sexual difference. This difference manifests itself in reciprocity, and in the recognition of the one sex to which *physis* entrusts birth: the undeniably feminine matrix of the appearance of humans on this earth.

Much as this is self-evident, it would be easier to express if thousands of years of patriarchal language had not encumbered the discourse of motherhood with pompous images of, and precepts about, mothers' nurturing/reproductive role. Still, it is necessary to take the risk of stumbling against this obstacle for the sake of attempting to steal – without much trouble – ancient figures who can restore signification to facts which demand it for what they are. Actually the purpose of the theft is to replace a theory that fails to affect our reality with a realistic one (Cavarero 1990: 93–121). Undeniably, the female gender is the site of regeneration for living humans of both sexes; the female sex, which is the same as the mother's, and the male, which is different. Therefore a dual order of gazes proceeds from the two sexes directed toward the mother. In their being either similar or different from her, the sexes acknowledge the reality that humans are bisexually differentiated, and that the common origin of both male and female is gendered in the feminine. Because the subject of the myth is the feminine matrix of all maternal power, the myth does not seem to thematize the son explicitly, nor the order of gazes between mother and son. It thematizes only the gazes exchanged between mother and daughter. Nevertheless the entire structure of the myth is really held in place by an implied and unspoken turning away (dis-traction) of the son's gaze from the mother. To put it differently, one might say that the myth, as always happens, and here especially, is structured on several levels of symbolic expression. The myth narrates explicitly the exchange of gazes between mother and daughter, which is forcibly interrupted by the abduction of the daughter by a masculine hand. But this narration conceals a withdrawal of the son's gaze from the mother, which, so to speak, might be regarded as "voluntary and pre-existing." The narration of the myth supports and determines this withdrawal. In fact the kernel of the myth is a disavowal of the maternal order of birth, an order that posits itself as a place from which human existence comes and takes signification. Instead, in the myth itself, signification chooses death as its measure, and this is hardly a coincidence. In this sense the myth evokes an original matricide. It is played out in two stages: the masculine gaze turns away from its own birth to look at its death; the gaze exchanged between mother and daughter is interrupted by a masculine hand.

Moreover, the erasure of the gaze between mother and daughter marks the privileged direction upon which matricide is carried out. Indeed, the mother sees and recognizes her gender in her daughter. And this gender is entrusted to a horizon of similarity that unfolds within the exchange of gazes between mothers and daughters, and is ultimately interwoven into all visual exchanges between women. Every woman comes from a mother and assures her mother of the possibility of perpetuating her gender, the figure of her being and embodiment. What follows is an interweaving of individual and hence different gazes, which exist in a common likeness already manifest at the outset: being of woman born. Right at the point where each female appears, sexual difference, which belongs to her gender, manifests itself to her and embraces her. Every woman is similar to her mother, even though they are also individually different. A daughter is neither yet a mother nor necessarily, in turn, a mother. The theme of this resemblance is not the necessity of imposing biological reproduction on women. It is the engendering that comes from maternal power and demands a reciprocity in the gaze that the newborn female returns to the mother.

In fact the myth is explicit: both the daughter who has been abducted from her mother and the earth itself grow sterile and no longer generate. When the mutual exchange of gazes between mother and daughter is denied, birth itself, *phyein*, ceases to happen. The female gender, in which birth is embodied, calls for a relationship of gazes between similarly female creatures. It demands that gender itself be a common horizon of recognition for every woman, so that birth, which has already happened, can (but does not have to) happen again. The symbolic figuration of the myth tells us that, between being mother and being woman, the fact of being born of mother cannot be cut off from the order of the female gaze where every woman, a daughter first, and only later, and not necessarily, a mother, finds her rootedness.

This point is of the utmost importance. It forbids the identification of the "substance" of being woman with the act of generating *alone* (that is, with the reductive identification of the feminine with the maternal, which patriarchal codes inscribe as a role). In my interpretation of the myth, and in the myth itself, maternal generation is just a root that welcomes the daughter within the horizon of similarity. In this sense of a common belonging the complicity of a secret that every woman shares at her discretion is transmitted through the feminine.

The myth says in fact that maternal power is the full power both to generate and not to generate: she does not have to generate, but she has generated already and she can generate again. This is because she carries in her womb the past and future infinity of human existence, as well as nothingness in the future sense of "no longer." And right here lies the deepest meaning of the feminine "secret" of life, which archaic cultures attribute to the Great Mother: to generate is an exclusively female experience, but it is not an automatic and obligatory process where women are mere vehicles.

To put it in more modern terms, the myth of Demeter reveals a sovereign figure of female subjectivity who decides, in the concrete singularity of every woman, whether or not to generate. For this sovereign figure, the act of generating is a prerogative rooted in her power – and therefore in her choice – to carry it out. It is not a duty imposed by a socially prescribed, external ethics supposedly inscribed in the law of nature. Quite to the contrary, far from being a force that prescribes an act of generation in which the mother is supposed to be an instrument, *physis* shows itself to be at one with the mother and to be rooted in her choice: the mother either assists or vetoes the birth that constitutes *physis*, not vice versa.

Thus the choice that belongs constitutively to maternal power carries within it, like all secrets, something truly dreadful: the possibility of nothingness, the annihilation of humankind, the desolation of the earth. This desolation is exactly what Demeter "produces" when her eyes grow desolate from the absence of her daughter's gaze, that is, the absence of an order of the female gaze, the symbolic horizon of the sovereignty of a woman's choice that is violently erased by the patriarchal order. The outright decision not to generate any more is a response to this erasure.

Certainly this is a dreadful reply; and yet it is the full and explicit manifestation of a power that can withstand acts of violence and injury, while still maintaining within itself a strength potentially more powerful than that of its opponents. This strength lies in reducing regeneration to nothingness (reducing the origin of being to nothingness). It is more powerful than the unbearable nothingness of death, the basis on which the patriarchal order categorizes all those born human as mortal.

Here, the order of the female gaze, which gives substance to maternal power, has definitely been damaged. With the complicity of other male deities, Hades kidnaps Kore and deports her to the realm of death. As I said in the beginning, no symbology is more explicitly bipolar in its design: an order of birth marked as feminine is opposed to an order of death marked as masculine.

The man snatches the daughter from the mother and takes her to his home. His is the house of unbearable death, the other face of the philosophy of eternity where the male philosopher finds his consolation. In the man's sorrowful dwelling where all beings born are called mortals, mother and daughter are now separated from each other and alone. Their gender can no longer take root and spread in their reciprocal gaze. Exiled to a masculine order, Kore is no longer Demeter's *daughter*, but Hades' *wife*, as her future sons and daughters will be Hades' children. The daughters will be destined to be wives of other men and objects of other deportations. The violence of this myth is not unusual or remote: the codes of modern society still carry it and inscribe it. The most manifest symptom of this legacy is the mechanism of family names, which even today are passed on from generation to generation on the paternal side.

So Kore is now motherless, and the daughters she might have are destined to be deported. She is now *alone*. The myth speaks of a periodic return of the female child to the mother. Therefore it is easy to interpret it through a system of agricultural symbols. A seed is hidden under the soil. In the spring it regenerates and grows, providing food. There is an ambiguity in how the context of the myth superimposes two different symbologies. On the one hand it evokes a mother/earth spontaneously generating fruit/children in the spring, and on the other a woman/field plowed by a man and fertilized by a masculine seed so that, in the right season, she can generate the son/fruit of the father (DuBois 1988: 39ff).[2] From yet another perspective, this passage of the myth also indicates the possibility of complicity between mothers and daughters, when mothers take care of their daughters' pregnancies and childbirth. Yet something more substantial is presented here which is far more important than the compromise of a periodical return to the mother.

There is a way in which women inhabit the patriarchal symbolic order that separates them from one another, leaves them on their own, having snatched them away from a place of common belonging and of mutual signification. This order relocates women in a place that assigns them roles and functions at the service of the fathers' realm. This is a place where women are "shadowy nurses" (Irigaray 1993b: 83). In this place, birthing, rearing, caring for, and feeding children are no longer acts inscribed in a feminine symbolic order capable of embracing them as secrets passed down through female genealogies; nor are they aspects of common experience inscribed in a feminine horizon. On the contrary, these acts are inscribed in an alien symbolic order that controls them, and, paradoxically, identifies them with the *nature* of the feminine. Here, nature, *physis*, is not the world's act of constituting itself, which is preserved for humans by a sovereign female subjectivity. It is instead a function ordered and controlled by the society of men.

Snatched away, cut off, and severed from the sovereign female subjectivity in which it is rooted, the power of maternity depreciates to mere reproductive function; a corporeal production of bodies. Obviously, these bodies are generated, nourished, and cared for. Indeed, here the corporeal dimension is prevalent, almost absolute: the mother is the container of the unborn child. Therefore she is apt to be controlled and is subject to domination by the order that has turned her into this receptacle. Hence the power of maternity is transformed into its opposite.

In this respect, the symbolic polysemy of the figure of Demeter is crucially significant in the different phases of the myth. In fact, there is a Demeter who regenerates in harmony with *physis* and within a system of the female gaze, and a Demeter who does not regenerate when this system is violated. In both cases, maternal power is complete, founded on a sovereign subjectivity that acknowledges the extent of its rootedness and claims the choice of regeneration as its own. There is also, however, a final phase in which Demeter "bends" to the compromise of her daughter's periodical return. Here the power of maternity begins to crack, and, not coincidentally, becomes inscribed within the regular rhythms of seasons, namely in a "natural" mechanism that gives the appearance of necessity. This mechanism seems to be in harmony with the female experience of menstrual cycles. Nevertheless it tends to represent the cycle itself not as the structural *condition* of a reproductive choice, but rather as a norm that requires and prescribes reproduction.

This final phase of the myth is the one that suffers most from the patriarchal order that seeks its expression in the myth itself. Besides, with its positive and negative valences, this phase is symbolically ambiguous in its representation of maternal power. Indeed, the act of generating still happens while the mother and the daughter are visible to each other. When this visibility is denied, Demeter does not regenerate. As a consequence, women's act of generating "by themselves" – which corresponds to the image of woman as mere reproductive function – is not yet clearly expressed here. Nevertheless it is evident that the final part of the myth shows the compromise between the order of birth and the order of death. It is true that it attempts to insert death (the seed under the ground) into a cycle of rebirths. But, significantly, it also designates death itself as the central locus of a masculine symbolic horizon.

Soon philosophy would build much more complex structures on death and its conceptualizations. But in this very ancient myth, it is symptomatic that the patriarchal order that violates the maternal order lives in the house of death. The parallels match almost too easily, but they are no less plausible for this reason. Men are excluded from the exclusively female experience of generating life (excluded from the secret). Since death takes away life, they find in death a place they regard as more powerful than life. Even so, the myth presents birth when it comes to a standstill, thereby indicating precisely the limits of this masculine strength.

From the masculine standpoint, it implies a revolution in perspective, which, in turn, initiates the crucial narrative passage of the myth. For man does not look at birth, at his being born of mother, which happens at the outset. He looks at death, and every time he prefigures his own death. This is not just a simple revolution in perspective, in which the tranquility of human rootedness yields to the intolerable grief of disappearance, where the beginning yields to the end. In other words, this operation affects the essential visibility of human bisexedness. This fact is manifest at the moment of birth from the mother.

Indeed when birth occurs one cannot fail to see sexual difference in the mother's sex and in the sex of the one who is born of her, who is always, incontrovertibly, either male or female. For "the child always has a sex. And it is, or would be a great crime to wish the child to be neutered. . . . As long as we live, we have a sex and are born of a sexedness" (Irigaray 1993b: 118).[3] On the contrary, when death occurs, sexual difference is not in the foreground. Indeed, men and women really die in their complete individuality. However, in death, the human place of sexedness and birth (which is feminine) is replaced by the solitary dissolution of the person who is dying into non-human, inorganic matter. Moreover, the masculine subject, who has chosen death as the site of *his* power and as the measure of earthly life, prefigures *his* own death in the anxiety at every death, and therefore sees it at the same time as *universal*, since it strikes everyone, and as *masculine*, for it will strike him.[4] Even the almost invulnerable Achylles died, because men, Man, inevitably die/s. Moreover, the whole world continuously dies, in the transience of every one of its beings.

The story of the universal masculine is quite old. It owes a lot to the shift in perspective that turns the patriarchal order toward death. In Homer's poems humankind is already named in the masculine plural. Symptomatically, humans are called "mortals." As we have already seen, this term – utilized, not coincidentally, by Parmenides and also very frequently by subsequent philosophers – distills the exact, particular traits of patriarchy, and, more specifically, prefigures the destiny of the West. We can see here both the centrality of death and the claim that masculinity is a universal valence. This expresses the absolute pretense that we have already mentioned: the masculine gender is made to denote the whole of humankind. And the place from which this gender speaks, a place that uproots humans from their maternal origin and therefore from *physis*, produces *metaphysics* as its supposed accomplishment. Metaphysics (a noun which is due to an accidental classification of Aristotle's works,[5] but is nonetheless more appropriate than any other) is not, in fact, a particular branch of philosophy. It is what permeates the language of Western culture, as it has developed beyond that ancient matricide: it is the adventure of a "spirit [that] in its perfection ... destroys its first roots. Its soil has become culture, history, which successfully forget that anything that conceives has its origins in the flesh" (Irigaray 1993b: 109). Metaphysics means that "mortals," but also "men," and, finally, "Man," signify men and women. For, in the order of *physis*, which the maternal figure protects and brings into the world, there is no woman who is a man, or might be designated in this way (as the maidservant from Thrace knew only too well). Man, with a masculine – universal – neutral valence, is a term from a language that has turned its gaze away from the place of birth, measuring existence on an end point that bears no memory of its beginning.

As it alone stands for the founding sense of all life, this end point throws open the anxiety of nothingness, and therefore forces one to look elsewhere – to a world not of this world – for the way out of the gulf chosen as the only horizon of an uprooted human existence. And the way out is nothing but the final act of approaching the metaphysical process, that is, the realm of thought to which men entrust their eternal and ultimately immortal essence, allowing the body, by now separate and inessential, to face its transient destiny.

Women's bodies will grow weary working for the bodies of those men. They will be reproductive shells, organs of nourishment and providers of care. These are elements of a "natural" process that anticipates roles that seem automatic and necessary but are in fact regulated from elsewhere. More specifically, they are regulated by the patriarchal order in a society that determines the ethical and legal codes of maternal generation.

A masculine symbolic horizon thus opens up. This horizon feeds on dualisms: woman/birth and man/death, body and thought. But these are uneasy dualisms. They are not bipolar opposites based on equality. For the masculine pole controls the other one; that is, the universalization of one sex reduces the other to a function, and throws all the negative categories upon it.

Consequently, in philosophy, the effect of this juxtaposition – like an undertow in the space between life and death – manifests itself in the way that death, as "a passing into nothingness," metaphysically determines that birth is "coming from nothing." The collective imagination which focuses, so to speak, on the subject of biology, also suffers from the establishment of the patriarchal order and a masculine perspective on birth. In specialized literature on this subject it is customary to find a distinction between the collective imaginations of antiquity and modernity. Supposedly, the first is "scientifically" naive, owing to its ignorance of the genetic mechanisms of reproduction. The ancients were apparently possessed by the kind of imagination that distorted the phenomenon of birth. The second is supposed to be more sophisticated owing to modern technical and scientific knowledge. Consequently, in the reasoning of these specialists, the modern imagination leaves very little space for imaginative distortion, and for any imaginative thought whatsoever, for that matter.

I do not believe, however, that things work this way. It seems to me, in fact, that in the archaic cultures characterized by the figure of the Great Mother a kind of *ignorance about genetics* produced a certain collective imagination. Later, this was forcibly replaced by another imagination produced by the *ignorance about genetics* that characterized classical Greece, a golden age for the patriarchal order. This is the kind of imagination that has been passed on to modern and contemporary times with no substantial variations in its symbolic message.

As classicists have often noted, the figure of the Great Mother is the foundation of the feminine origin of life. But this is not simply based on the acknowledgment of the incontrovertible fact of giving birth. It is also built on the kind of ignorance about reproductive mechanisms that attributes to women an absolute power to create life by themselves. This valence is a "secret," a completely feminine secret, for in this imaginative frame the act of mating with a man nine months prior to birth is not connected with the birth itself. This ignorance of the genetic fact of conception reinforces the power of maternity. The result is that the experiences of gestation and childbirth are placed in a realistic light, and these facts are exclusively feminine.

With the stabilization of the patriarchal symbolic order, a reverse kind of ignorance about genetics is set up, a reversal that has crucial significance. It attributes to the father alone the substance of the power to generate. In fact, in Aristotle's doctrine, which summarizes previous opinions on the subject, it is affirmed that the maternal womb contains inert and cold matter to which the warm sperm gives life and form (Sissa 1983: 81–145). This whole argument is presented in a language marked by convention, according to which, in the final analysis, the maternal womb, if well activated by vigorous sperm, ends up functioning like a little oven.[6] This shows that the image of the mother/container goes hand in hand with the theory of "maternity as nurture," according to which the mother is merely a passive element, apt to be devoured (Sissa 1983: 103). Demeter, who gives food since she is the mother, already bespeaks Plato.

In this ancient embryology of patriarchal foundation, the maternal power to generate life was transformed into a transitional site on the way to a life generated by fathers, into a nurturing cell. Breastfeeding is a continuation and a confirmation of this power. As Apollo forcefully affirms in the *Eumenides* (274. 665–71):

> The mother is not the generator of what we call the generated, her child. On the contrary, she is just a nurse to the fetus with which she is inseminated. The generator is the one who scatters the seed; the mother is like a host to the guest: she simply welcomes and keeps the sprout, lest both are damaged by some deity.

Ignorance about genetics reveals itself here too for what it is. It functions in support of the symbolic order that substantiates it. This is the symbolic order that patriarchal society now founds on the concept of death (the divine "damage" to human growth).

Indeed birth is recuperated within a biological matrix that is exclusively masculine. Far from constituting the manifestation of human existence in the world in its individual wholeness, the significance of birth is already reduced to the body. Consequently, birth "provides" the transient part of a human being, the body, for human excellence is to be found in the intellectual part of the soul. In sum, the living human being has been split into body and intellect: and, more specifically, into a body destined to die and into an intellect capable of contemplating the eternal. So, on the one hand, the body, which is destined to die, draws even its birth from the grief of death. On the other hand, the intellect, which is consubstantial with the eternal, has no beginning and therefore no end.

And so truly it is the *theory* of birth which got lost as a consequence of the consolidation of this new ignorance about genetics. In the first place, it happened with the imposed perception of the mother as a temporary container rather than as the origin of life, and as a nutritional apparatus for new bodies both born and unborn. In the second place, birth ceased to bring into the world living beings who lived their lives to the fullest and in a unity of mind and body. Birth was limited instead to providing humans with a body, which came from the paternal loins, while their intellect emerged and lived in disembodied regions.

Birth is subjected to a loss of meaning as the result of the ancient matricide. Having uprooted itself from *physis*, the fathers' metaphysical order claims control over matter. Having been reduced to the feminine vehicle of a reproductive process, the power of maternity is regulated by public norms within the paternal order. From Aristotle's conjectures to modern embryology, science has made relentless progress in acknowledging "equal" roles for ovum and sperm at conception. The symbolic frame remains nonetheless the same, though rendered more complicated by an insane acceleration of manipulative techniques. These carry with them a developing system of norms increasingly invasive of woman's body.

The basic coordinates of this symbolic framework are simple: the function of maternity is reproductive, and the function of reproduction is social. Both are made to belong to the realm of human cohabitation, and both are a matter of public interest that can be regulated by laws. This has an even simpler consequence: politically organized society continues to claim that maternal nurturing is to be taken for granted and will be provided in the form of unpaid household labor and caregiving.

If we restrict our focus to the theme of public interest in the functions of maternity and reproduction, we can schematically outline two aspects of legislation and jurisprudence where this theme is manifest: the area of demographic stability, which concerns society in general, and the area of the rights of the unborn, which concerns the human person as subject of constitutionally protected rights.

Obviously, public intervention differs in kind depending on which one of the two areas is being considered. Indeed demographic problems are rarely the object of direct coercive regulations.[7] These reached their peak with the Nazis and their atrocious "eugenics" (Bock 1992: 89–109). Intervention happens more frequently through propaganda campaigns that encourage and reward maternity – even economically. In these circumstances, the function of maternity is completely social. In general, it amounts to providing the fatherland with sons, and industry with manpower. In any case, it is treated as a function needing regulation, through either an increase or a decrease in production, according to the demands of society or the market (Del Re 1989: 119–47). According to this logic, to leave demographic issues to any single woman's sovereign choice, and to her freedom to decide about her maternal experience, would be contrary both to a maternal power reduced to social function, and to a public interest claiming to be *universal*; this interest, nonetheless, models itself precisely on the masculine it has adopted as neutral/universal. To put it briefly, the problem is how to regulate the flow of new citizens. Since women are the ones who produce citizens, this production must be guided, planned, and controlled. The uterus may no longer be the "little oven" of old in which the paternal gene was nurtured and cozily leavened; it still looks a lot like it, however.

On the other hand, the problem of the unborn child as the subject of legal rights falls squarely within the realm of public legislation. It has to do primarily with voluntary abortion, that is control of the reproductive function when conception has already happened. This control is designed to prevent the pregnant woman from eventually making a decision not to procreate, or at least to place normative limitations in the way of this decision. When we have demographic control, the intervention happens "upstream," as it were. Birth control transforms the mother's power to procreate or not into a useful and externally regulated function. When the issue is voluntary abortion, the law intervenes "downstream," so to speak, radically reducing the pregnant woman's ability to decide autonomously whether to procreate or not. Consequently, maternity is not merely a reproductive function; here it is also a social function separate and separable from the subject who "carries" it. (Host to the guest, as Apollo proclaimed!)

This is most manifest in legislation that completely outlaws voluntary abortion. But it is also implied in laws that regulate it by envisaging ways and contexts in which a woman's decision to have an abortion must be made. In either case, the fact that the woman wants to abort is never presented as a question of women's free choice (to be followed automatically by the medical assistance the woman requires). From the beginning, the issue of abortion is political. It is a concern of the state that is regulated by the laws of the nation. It is above all an issue of the law, which fluctuates embarrassingly between ethics and metaphysics.

Indeed, once the act of regeneration has been pulled out of the sovereign space of maternal power (once this power has been reduced to a reproductive function), to separate the unborn child/embryo from the mother/container is an easy logical step. It assumes that definitions of the concept of "man" as biological human species (which are evidently extra-juridical in their substance) can be extended to the embryo, already an individual, identifiable genetically within its species, and therefore entitled to the constitutional rights granted to *men*. In the final analysis, this logic implies a definition of the concept of "life," which is not content with designating only the already born (whom we all have in mind when we speak of the living), and therefore ventures to apply itself to the embryonic process.

The problem is whether or not the human embryo (also classified as fetus by medical science) is a juridical subject and therefore falls within the body of legislation that regulates the community of the living. Is this embryo just a possibility of life, or a being *already* living in the maternal womb? This question obviously manifests the preoccupation with establishing how to substantiate the existence of a future citizen's individual identity in the intrauterine phase. For, from the beginning this individual "is a man" in a context in which all men are citizens. In other words, if those who participate in the community of the living are the living members of the human species, and are thus assumed to be juridical subjects, then, to the extent that the embryo falls under the concept of the living, it is already a juridical subject. It is a subject contained within (and nourished by) another subject.

The language of the law is emblematic on this point. It goes as far as to articulate statements that define the pregnant woman as a "remarkable *armor* that protects the development of the fetus until it is viable." Just as remarkable is the perception of the relationship between mother and fetus as one between companions sharing the same food (Traverso 1977: 10).

When the rights of the unborn and the rights of the mother are mapped out in these terms, they clash if the mother decides to have an abortion. This conflict triggers a scenario where a stronger subject (the mother) is pitted against a weaker subject (the unborn). The unborn is the subject that the political/juridical community must protect, even more so for the very fact that it is weaker.

The metaphysical bedrock of the law can be broken down into a cluster of questions. A crucial issue is deciding *when* the embryo becomes a juridical subject – in which month of pregnancy it has already become a living individual. As such, the embryo would fall under the tutelage of a common law that implicates all living people in a public sphere regulated by common norms. This argument is organized in such a way that, if the point is internal consistency, the best answer is that the subjectivity of the embryo/fetus/unborn child can be regulated from the time of conception. In fact, there is no logical reason to assume that the unborn child becomes a juridical subject (an individual equipped with a personal identity) in a certain month of gestation. Indeed, the reasoning that suggests this is not based on a logical consistency; it is founded on the practical experience of common living, where logical reasoning tacitly comes to terms with the "phenomenon" of abortion, which is irrepressible.

Certainly there is another argument based on more realistic considerations. It suggests that a being can be considered living (and therefore a subject of law) when it is capable of autonomous life *separately* from the maternal womb. But this means considering the mother and the unborn child inseparable. Thereby, it subverts the logic organized on the basis of the prejudice that the unborn child and the mother/container are separable. Indeed, the crucial point is establishing the distinction between a woman and her reproductive function a priori of any legal considerations. The suggestion implied in the current logic is that, of course, as a citizen, a woman is supposed to be a full juridical subject, but, as a pregnant person, she is the container of the unborn child. As things stand, in sum, neither her womb nor what is happening in it belong to her, so that the decision to generate is not hers. The act of engendering from maternal power is a concern of the state which might admit a female choice, but only within pre-established modalities and limiting statutes.

The modern techniques that render *visible* the inside of the body of the pregnant woman have certainly contributed to producing a cultural anxiety of separation that aligns the woman, the uterus, and the embryo in a nice logical order.[8] One has only to think of how influential the likeness between a human shape and the shape of an unborn child is in establishing that the fetus becomes a subject of law at a certain month of pregnancy. Indeed, both voluntary and spontaneous abortions (as well as autopsies) have since time immemorial displayed fetuses at various stages of pregnancy eternalized in glass jars. But one should not underestimate the impact of this new monitored visibility, easily accessible on an everyday basis. On the screen the uterus is a colored aura, shaped like a vase and rendered separate from the female body by a frame that focuses on the womb. In this mere receptacle, by contrast, the fetus is visible in its entirety.

The visibility of the inside of a woman's body is indeed the most evident symptom of a massive *invasion* of the female body by modern techniques, both gynecological and genetic. As happens with most things, this too has a positive aspect: the well-meaning intent of medical science to prevent illness and deliver health care. But this aspect runs the risk of being eclipsed and giving way to an invasive and manipulative obsession that uses the female body as an area of experimentation where birth is increasingly constructed as an event detached from the mother's experience. This obsession treats wombs, ova, and sperms as separate and combinable elements. Its inevitable and pernicious result is that *scientific invasiveness* carries with it a sort of *juridical invasiveness*, which is consistently inscribed in the larger phenomenon of the juridification of the lifeworld that characterizes contemporary society (Habermas 1987: 368ff). At this point, a legislator might be expected to set standards for situations in which it can be both paradoxically difficult and symptomatically problematical to establish who is the mother of the child, either born or unborn. Clearly, if one can find in three separate places a refrigerated fertilized ovum, the woman from whom the ovum was taken, and another woman who accepts the ovum into her uterus and "hatches" it, then the genetic imagination of antiquity, although revised and modified, can very well take pride in the theory of the *little oven*. Here, with a truly artistic touch for separation and recombination, some imaginative variety is added to the distinction between conception and uterus/receptacle.

Regardless of how the law addresses the problem, it is clear that by now birth has been removed not only from the sovereignty of maternal power but also from the basic feminine experience of maternity. Here indeed not only maternity, understood as reproductive function, and the fetus, understood as a legal subject, are concerns of the state, but so is the ovum, in its aseptic separateness and unpredictable wanderings through more or less compliant wombs.

This is a paradoxical scenario, and it becomes even more so every day owing to the rapid development of manipulative techniques. It appears, however, that the sovereign subjectivity of maternal power, shaped by the ancient figure of Demeter, has had the strength to survive even through these bleak millennia of captivity. The bare fact that women decide to have abortions and manage to get them is an unvarnished reality which proves that a great many women, from time immemorial and in all parts of the world, know themselves to be sovereign subjects of maternal power, despite all sorts of juridical invasiveness. Their decision demonstrates that the choice is entirely and intimately theirs. It is never a concern of the state, either where completely prohibitive regulations prevail or where more liberal provisions and procedures are in place. Risking their lives and breaking the law, or, more precisely, risking their lives because they are breaking the law, women demonstrate that they know that maternity is indeed their own concern, not an issue of public law. It is a question of the irreducible individuality of every woman as a living whole made of body and mind. When having an abortion, a woman demonstrates that she experiences herself as a whole, put at risk in its *entirety* by maternity, even though scientific and legal invasiveness is eager to turn the focus of attention away from the female mind and body. When she decides to have an abortion she decides for *herself* and for *no one else* (she does not decide for the embryo that as such is still within her body, not yet born). In any case, she is alone and entirely responsible for her decision.

Moreover, the state seems to acknowledge this fact when it bends the metaphysical logic of the unborn child as a legal subject to a temporal calculation of how this subjectivity can be assumed. Hence it allows voluntary abortion within the first three months of pregnancy, thereby deciding (with a logically inconsistent argument) that the fetus does not become "other" immediately after conception, but only at a certain point in time during its development. Thereafter it is a juridical subject that can be placed under the tutelage of the state, even *against* its own mother. Here, evidently, metaphysics gives way to some kind of compromise between the unsurmountable fact of sovereign maternal power and the collective patriarchal codes.

But compromises, while sometimes useful and acceptable, are always counterproductive if they are ultimately sustained by the original matricide. The violence against Demeter continues. Her injured body (*physis*) cannot content itself with a merely symbolic survival in the testimony of clandestine abortions, or in the partial compromises conceded by the law. More than any other, the ancient figure of Demeter seems therefore to demand a new philosophy of birth capable of winning some territory back from the metaphysics of death and from the social codes built upon it.

Plato would say that this is not as easy as turning over a shell. The shift in perspective, the new way of measuring the sense of human existence on birth rather than death, cannot be brought about simply by replacing the negative with the positive in reverse parallelism. It must do battle with an already invaded territory where the occupying forces seem to be advancing boldly rather than considering retreat.

In other words, it seems that the best response to the original matricide and the violation of the order of birth is to counterattack this *invasion* with a *withdrawal*, rather than to work toward compromise (which nonetheless brings some practical advantages with respect to laws that completely outlaw abortion). When the maternal power with respect to generation is juxtaposed with the invasiveness of the law, it becomes a site that *per se* resists any regulation. In short, the issue is how to redefine the experience of maternity and the range of decisions inherent in it, as a space free from juridical power, a *rechtsfreier Raum*, as described in the incisive words of a recent study by Arthur Kaufmann, a German legal theorist (1990: 13–16). Or at least, in more traditional though still risky terms, it is a matter of defining maternal power as a right whose norms cannot be arbitrarily negotiated, or compared with other juridical situations.

Basically, it is a matter of accepting the sovereignty of maternal subjectivity, as witnessed everywhere down through the millennia of chosen abortions. This fact can be inscribed in an order of birth that interrogates the legitimacy of being regulated by a social order founded on the centralization of death. The crucial question therefore is not how to negotiate or improve the regulations on voluntary abortion but how to come to a general consensus that maternal power *per se* cannot be regulated. The women's movement has called all this the "decriminalization of abortion," signifying both a woman's understandable desire to avoid the penalties envisaged for transgressing regulations on abortion and, more importantly, the desire to place women's power to generate or not to generate outside the sphere of any negotiable regulations.

In the wake of the solemn tone of the myth of Demeter, it seems reductive to invoke the crude fact of elective abortion as a way of reaffirming the just claims of the violated order of birth. Still, the reality of abortion is a crucial indicator that a sovereign maternal subjectivity is manifest even in captivity. At the same time this reality emblematically demonstrates the arrogance of legal invasiveness, the glamour of its metaphysical pretensions, contradictory logic, and Aristotelian lineage. The practice of abortion is an important indicator that opens up the issue of a silenced and misrepresented maternal power. It demands a philosophy of birth capable of giving voice to this power; a voice that acknowledges the dignity of being alive (as either woman or man), thanks to our common maternal origin, before our social integration into the fathers' political order.

Indeed the kind of revolution in perspective where the symbolic axis shifts from death to birth implies a global rethinking of the meaning of the world that would reach well beyond a simple claim of female autonomy in the matter of abortion. In fact, an immense symbolic structure has developed upon the centrality of the category of death. It is founded on an initial abstraction of thought from *physis*, shifting it beyond (*meta*)physics. This structure has cut off the concrete roots of life, banishing humans and the meaning of their lives into patriarchal exile, into a society that claims to provide a code that regulates the entire world. We could say schematically that this operation subsumes the meaning of life into the category of societal existence. This involves a complete absorption of "disembodied" living humans into the political realm, leaving no trace behind. Even a glance at the doctrine of Aristotle and Plato on the subject is enough for us to realize how politics constitutes the purpose and fulfillment of those humans who lack a nonpolitical/apolitical *elsewhere* that gives them substance. In their case, this *elsewhere* is indeed a mere embodiedness, insignificant precisely because it is nonpolitical or apolitical. Aristotle's view is peremptory on this matter: outside the political order that absorbs humans and gives them reality, the individual is not a man, but a beast or a god (*Politics* 1253a). Furthermore, for Aristotle, the same political order assigns to every human his or her "natural" place and function. On the one hand, it places women and slaves in the realm of domesticity where bodies are nurtured even though their existence is insignificant; on the other it assigns free adult males to the government of the *polis*, where the disembodied human soul fulfills its own purpose. Certainly this understanding of politics undergoes major changes in the course of Western history and most of all in the modern era. But the main idea remains that the political horizon is absolute and totalizing, at the expense of a sense of life rooted *before* and *elsewhere*; that is, at the expense of a meaning of human existence not *immediately* and *completely* subject to public regulation, and thereby invaded by societal codes. All the more so since the centrality of death holds together these codes founded by Hades – abductor of the daughters – thereby producing the erasure of birth that renders life a "boundless" land subject to invasion.

As a recuperation of the sense of human engendering from the mother, a philosophy of birth has thus the main purpose of disinvesting the concrete individuality of each human from societal totalization. Birth, love, and death belong irreducibly to humans, despite state claims that they are legal matters subject to regulation. These experiences are rooted precisely in the singularity of a lived personal life that the public sphere has always wanted to absorb into codes and regulations. But turning the gaze toward the mother, one can acknowledge that these are separate from the site of negotiable common living, and not subject to societal regulation. They are *physis* rather than *polis*.

Here *physis* means birth, as befits its etymological origin. As I have already mentioned, contrary to death, in birth one is not alone but in a duo: the mother and the one who is born. Birth is therefore inevitably a relationship between unequals. The one who is born, the living human, is here already, is already *to be found*. Certainly, the newborn is unrepeatably "new," it is a re-present-ation (a making eternally present) of the "beginning" that inscribes its own being in every living creature that came into the world to begin and not to die (Arendt 1959: 154ff). However, in its singularity the newborn is a "beginning" found already "started" inside the mother: it is generated by the female who has already been generated by a m/other, and so on *ad infinitum* in a sequence (*theoria*) of past mothers. Therefore the innocent contingency of being "here and now, thus and not otherwise" belongs constitutively to those who are born and alive, coming from their mother in an infinite series of the engendered, of new beginnings unfolding in reverse progression. The sense of being or having been born is found precisely in this discovery of the self in the world of individual existence.

Basically, it is a matter of placing oneself within a perspective from which the existing individual observes his/her own self, but not from the bewildered isolation of one who is simply there and clings to existence expecting it to last. On the contrary, s/he looks in the direction from which s/he came, as a presence that was revealed from a given starting point. Therefore s/he understands that her/his *being there already* does not originate from the self, does not find its substance there. It comes from her who has decided to bring this child into the world, so that the child can find for itself a place in this world. Finitude, contingency, and irreducibility are the signs of this new perspective that looks toward the origin of the living individual to find its own measure, and not toward its fateful end.

It is one thing to describe humans as *finite*, or destined to die. It is quite another to describe their finitude as a sense of being brought into the world as a result of a mother's decision. These individuals have already appeared at a beginning point where nothing of their singularity had yet been determined, even though all of it was already irrevocably given. Indeed, in this case finitude is the particular and determined "here and now" of my own existence. It involves everything that is accidental (but in fact irreversible) in finding myself to be the way I am. I am first of all a whole of mind and body, a female living person gendered in difference. Next I am situated in this space, at this time, and in this corner of the world to which my mother is *the* threshold.

This is indeed the *irreducible* concreteness of which I am made, and with which I am at one. This kind of irreduciblity demands that it not be *reduced* to an abstract paradigm determined within the realm of societal cohabitation. Like all facts, it demands a meaning that does not disavow its reality. Therefore I will be this woman or this man, never *man*. And I will be this immediately and forever, a whole made of mind and body *never* divisible into "superfluous matter" and "essential thought." The natal relationship of every human to her/his mother is unbalanced since accident, innocence, and indebtedness are intertwined within it. It is other, or distant from the relationship that every human has with any other human, for mother and child share a living space, in which it is useful for them to establish norms of common living.

So by focusing on the category of birth, it is possible to restore meaning both to maternal power and to the reality of those who are born. This focus is a kind of "return" to Demeter. To be more specific, it involves bringing to the foreground the field in which this figure was stolen. Indeed, in birth we always find a woman who generates. This beginning is decided upon, and therefore expresses a sovereign subjectivity inscribed in the act of regeneration which belongs to the *physis* rather than the *polis*. But in birth we also have the one who is generated. The one who is born comes to measure the concreteness of being in the world, in this way and not otherwise, in a process of birth through which s/he first appears in the world as a whole. Certainly, the one who is born also belongs to the *polis*, and will have to live with others (both female and male) according to common rules, probably negotiated, contingent, and revisable. But these rules will not aim at defining what belongs to the secret of the natal relationship, a secret that takes the form of a mother's decision bequeathed by nature to the origin of every living human before social integration.

Therefore a significant result of the philosophical shift in perspective on birth is a narrowing of the societal sphere. This sets limits on both legislation and the political symbolic order, which must divest itself of its totalizing and evangelizing aims, allowing the meaning of human life to exist outside the confines of the *polis*. Within its confines it will be possible to negotiate rules and objectives of common living, in the awareness that the negotiators are not "men," not the abstract, universal individuals of legal discourse, but very concrete men and women rooted in a different kind of sexedness since they come into the world gendered in one way or the other. They are also differentiated in a thousand other ways that bind them to the specific options and interests that inevitably inform the idea of a just community of living persons. On the other hand, these options and interests are tied up with a *being there already* that, far from happening in a void or coming out of nothing, actually takes place in the historically determined space and time that constitute one's *biographical conditioning*. It is thus understood that, before being a citizen, everyone is a human born of mother, and every mother is such above and beyond being a citizen. For, in the *polis* she does not negotiate the maternal power that concretely belongs to her sex, nor does she allow others to negotiate it.

Therefore there is indeed a home for Penelope, where a living individual can take root and find meaning; there is a boundary that demands an absolute separation between *home* and *polis*. In the mythic figure of Penelope the act of disinvestment from the *polis* must be irrevocable, so that she can exist in a separate and impenetrable space. Moreover, the symbolic effectiveness of the figure of Penelope lies in this absolute "separatism." In fact, when we *begin* from the space of the vital sign of female subjectivity, we draw a boundary that restricts the patriarchal political order through a process of reappropriation. Penelope does not redefine the *polis*, she simply allows the *polis* to be elsewhere and not to touch, not to invade, her home. In this sense Penelope's act is crucial to constructing a female space and indicating its primacy, despite, against and separate from the patriarchal *polis*. And nevertheless starting from this home of the living where meaning is returned to being born of woman, nothing prevents the imagining of another *polis*, a space where the rules of common living are found through the concrete matter that concerns it.

In other words, when the home designed by Penelope has gathered enough strength to ensure its survival and to prove itself as a space free from any societal invasion, it is possible that this force will take on the task of redefining the *polis*. It will no longer be constituted as just an exercise in masculinity where "man" power is displayed, but rather also as an arena where concrete individuals live together.

The picture is not ideal, since the newly defined *polis* is only an imagined potential, while the patriarchal *polis*, even in its modern democratic guise, is already in place and weighs upon us. It is a question of deciding whether or not an anomalous and theoretically explosive philosophy of birth needs to become a way of rethinking the entire world, including the category of communal living; whether or not it can attack the patriarchal order on its impervious terrain. There is no doubt that the patriarchal order has prepared a hostile territory: both history and laws are masculine/universal; mothers negotiate on the basis of rules established by a matricidal culture; and sexed human beings are neutral, abstract "humans" connoted as male. Therefore, to make this territory accessible to the few women who choose to enter it, an invasion by the anomalous female symbolic order is necessary. Nonetheless the invaders run the unavoidable risk of being coopted by the fictitious "neutral" male, of feeling estranged and alienated. The tactics of this invasion are worthy of the ancient Amazons, juxtaposing the nimbleness of an unpredictable incursion with the millennial patriarchal occupation. We female invaders are organized in small units. We come "with a different territorial map than the one they planned to hand us" (Putino 1988: 13), and we find our home, our strength elsewhere, precisely in that space that has been shaped by our retreat. Our retreat quickly turns into an incursion in order to completely take back the order of birth that claims this contingent strategy as its own. In the effort to restrict the boundaries of the *polis* we put into practice rules that are finally free from the universalizing claims of abstract totalization.

Perhaps, according to the metaphysical play of light and darkness facilitated by the myth of Demeter, a reshaped "city of the sun" will be inhabited by men and women who remember their being in the world as a "coming into the light," whether as females or males, born of mother.

The juridification of the lifeworld is only the most evident, tangible aspect of society's invasion of the symbolic order of birth, an invasion that has been nurtured and sustained by metaphysics and ethics (secular and otherwise) down through the millennia. Recently, the new discipline of bioethics seems to have joined forces with these fields, while it also has some particular expectations.

It is difficult to give a precise definition of the various meanings attributed to bioethics, but its "historical" motivations are easy to investigate. Scientific experimentation has invaded the realm of life (*bios*), bringing the law with it. This raises a question on the limits of such invasiveness. The answer is left to bioethics. Obviously, those who provide answers are "experts," mostly philosophers and theologians. Jurists, however, also lend a hand. This should not be surprising: they have long been familiar with the field of *bios*, having produced laws on abortion. By now they are "connoisseurs" in good standing, because the limitations imposed by ethics must also be translated into public laws in order to be effective and respected by scientists.

Bioethics is also concerned with euthanasia and animal rights. However, abortion, artificial insemination, and genetic manipulation are its major interests. These are particularly significant because they are inscribed in the female body as a site of scientific experimentation. In short, the uterus is a laboratory and the event of birth provides material for experimentation.

Given its name, it would seem that within bioethics it is the category of *bios* that determines the limits of what scientific action can be attempted. Therefore, in bioethics, everything is played out on the meaning attributed to the word "life." Indeed life observes itself here, but it does so with the son's distracted gaze. Maternal life-giving power remains hidden. Consequently, according to the overused strategies of the matricidal tradition, life itself becomes the kind of phenomenon where the maternal womb is merely a technical vehicle for the assemblage of multiple, controllable elements. Once again, with the forced eclipse of maternal subjectivity, the living human is viewed for the genetic material out of which s/he is (pre)fabricated. In the case of abortion, the question is again spelled out in metaphysical language. From what point onward is this genetic material already a living individual, ethically intangible in his/her human dignity and therefore entitled to legal protection? Obviously, as we already know, the answer can only be an educated guess, or a "reasonable" compromise with genetic manipulation which is in fact already practiced in the laboratory.

Indeed it is science that leads the way, or to be more specific the kind of scientific progress that advances only in reference to itself and its power. Only *later* it encounters the ethical question of whether or not it is right and legitimate to do what it does. The question is a thorny one, since by definition both *progress* and the scientific myth that sustains it *move forward* in linear progression, and neither will readily look "back." This is all the more true if the precepts of the world-view based on scientific progress collude either to keep "progress" moving forward or to hold it back. In my view this play on the word "progress" indicates that, if maternal power has been erased *from the start* and reduced to a reproductive function of the womb, then all restrictions on invading *bios* are removed; the symbolic order where living creatures find a secret, protected, maternal home has been cancelled. This is one of the great many meanings of the secret of birth: birth is not what cannot be explained "scientifically," but the symbolic figure declared inviolable by maternal power.

In order to impose bioethical limitations on scientific experiments, it seems useless to resort to the principles of the very same culture (however reformulated, corrected, or even regretted) that is founded on a boundless violation of its own natal biological order. It is necessary to resort to a different symbolic arrangement that promises to take better care of the order of birth inscribed in life, so that bioethics can again take on the meaning of its ancient root, so impudently invoked in modern languages. For if *bios* indeed belongs to *physis*, when the meaning of *physis* as "birth" is restored, then *bios* too will find a meaning for which it is appropriate to suggest an *ethos*.

Women often justifiably raise their voices in protest against bioethics "ignoring the female subject" (Mancina 1987: 17; Fattorini 1987: 9–12). But this lack of attention is indeed only a macroscopic indicator and logical consequence of the symbolic matricide that happens when the son predictably turns his gaze away from the mother. In my analysis of Demeter's myth, I note that birth calls for a dual system of the gaze: one between the mother and the daughter, the other between the mother and the son. It is because in the myth of origin the son decides to dis-tract himself and turn his attention to death, exiling the daughter there, that the gaze between the mother and the daughter is forcibly interrupted. Therefore, after this act, in the patriarchal symbolic order, neither the son nor the daughter look at the mother, the *physis*. But while the son can decide to do so, the daughter has been violently prevented from looking. Bioethics cannot then develop as a meaningful science if it does not acknowledge the "ethical fault" (Irigaray 1993b: 122) of the son against *bios* that has rendered the meaning of *physis* invisible.

There is, therefore, a great need for bioethics. But it appears that the daughter, rather than the son, is in a position to claim its voice. In retrieving the once interrupted gaze of the mother, she who has innocently experienced – and still experiences – the warped and downtrodden order of birth brings back to light an experience of *bios* far better than the one of self-proclaimed "experts." Thus the limiting of scientific modes of operating is not intended to bar or to censure a progression. They are a new disinvestment from the order of death, claiming that the life which, by its own *nature*, was such from the beginning is not subject to invasion. Within this original horizon of *physis* protected by maternal power, bioethics becomes the more or less appropriate name for ethics. Indeed *ethos* is about action, and action is the agency of individuals who orient themselves into the world, as they begin their lives having been born from a mother.

It is not easy to deal with ethical issues in detail nor to give its problems practical resolutions. Nonetheless in this new symbolic horizon it becomes both possible and meaningful "to elaborate a culture based on the acceptance of human limitation, where insuperable boundaries" within which science must operate can be successfully established (Vegetti Finzi 1987: 13).

On the other hand, an aspect of this science that transforms ova and embryos with results as amazing as those of alchemy appears to be primarily "at the disposal" of women's desire for maternity. Through its techniques, women who are infertile for various technical reasons either become mothers in the proper biological sense, or they have their inseminated ova implanted in a "host" woman, according to a modernized version of Apollo's ancient motto. Beyond the already mentioned legal problems this implies, one must ask which symbolic female figure can sustain this desire to be a mother at any price.

Indeed, one could reasonably maintain that here science does nothing but respond to a feminine demand. Still the point is to question precisely the obsessive desire by which this demand is sustained. This desire of a woman to be a mother crucially reveals the totalizing coincidence of feminine identity with its maternal role, so that if a woman cannot be a mother something essential is denied: her value, function, role. Indeed, since the patriarchal codes have decided that women totally consist in this preordained role, obviously a great many women are conditioned to attach themselves to it. What other *space* of positive self-recognition do these codes concede to women outside this assigned *place*, if not the complementary role of virgin (Irigaray 1993b: 72)?[9]

Through the figure of Demeter, it is therefore crucial to trace again a feminine symbolic order in which maternity itself can be a space, not a "place." Most of all it is necessary to outline a space from which we come and toward which we look with a *daughter's* eyes, according to the order of reality prior to the symbolic, in which every female human is born a daughter before she becomes a mother. The desire to become a mother may certainly be strong, yet it cannot have the coercive force of a desire that corresponds to one's only conceded identity (and indeed a warped identity, inasmuch as it is defined by the distracted son). But it has the force of one who has chosen to repeat the maternal experience that her own mother has not imposed on her. In short, in the reciprocal gaze exchanged between mother and daughter, the figure of maternity is already complete on both sides, the generator and the generated. Yet no sense of duty forces the daughter into the desire to generate and if perchance this desire is eventually thwarted, the frustration can be borne with quiet regret. Indeed, maternal power, as a symbolic site of human origin assigned to the female gender, is not denied to any daughter who wants to keep her gaze on the mother. But within the patriarchal order that wants to prevent this gaze, the daughter is left alone without a theory of the feminine. Becoming a mother may be for her the only means to look at maternity as the most direct form of personal incarnation.

If, as bioethics, ethics has certain analytical methods, then each child who is born as a daughter is entitled to recognize herself as such in the female gender. She can thus take her direction from a sense of rootedness in a human mother, something already given that no one can take away. It might seem paradoxical, but indeed in this perspective, founded on maternal power, an apprenticeship in being a daughter is necessary first of all, so that her desire to be a mother can become rooted in a free subjectivity rather than ordered by the father and the son's code. They have many representative figures in the patriarchal symbolic order; they are even capable of devoutly mentioning the Mother of the Son. But they rarely mention the mother of the daughter, and even less these two women's reciprocal gaze. Therefore, the primeval mother/daughter couple staged by the myth of Demeter has the merit of naming a mother who not only posits her relationship with her daughter as primary, but, more importantly, wants her daughter to be what she is. Demeter wants Kore who is a girl, the virgin to whom she has given birth. She does not want a pregnant daughter in an uninterrupted act of regeneration.[10]

If we begin from this horizon of a feminine gender that knows about origins and mediation, the desire to be the mother of a daughter is possible and even probable. However, it is difficult to see it reflected in the spectacle of possible embryos, which will be scientifically developed and placed on the market at women's disposal, at any price. These perpetuate the reproductive role forcibly thrust on female identity, even though they purport to offer a remedy for its unbearable frustrations.

4

Diotima

I once heard an account from a Mantinean woman
named Diotima who was wise and skillful in this
and many other things. At one time, by having the
Athenians offer sacrifices before the plague occurred,
she produced a ten-year postponement of the disease for
them, and she instructed me in the activities of Love.
I'll try as well as I can to repeat her account for you on
my own.

Plato, *Symposium* 201d

A priestess and foreigner, Diotima of Mantinea is a woman wise
on the subject of Love and many other matters. Her situation is
the reverse of that of the Thracian maidservant, though they are
both of the same sex. In Diotima's case, it is not her comeliness,
wit, or teasing "ignorance" that stands out, but her solemn
wisdom. In contrast with the slave girl's quick words of retort,
echoing with laughter, Diotima offers a long philosophical speech
that is fully consonant with Plato's thought. In fact it is one of
the highest expressions of that philosophy. Occasionally Diotima
tempers her severity with subtle irony. Yet her humor does not
display itself in a burst of laughter. It feels rather like of a teacher's

benevolent smile, as Diotima points out to Socrates, her most outstanding student, the error of his contradictory thinking, and thus leads him back to a more coherent way of arguing

Diotima is indeed a teacher. She possesses knowledge, and leads her pupil toward it, so that he too can understand and share it. This knowledge is directed upward, in a gradual ascending movement that leads the mind's eye away from the things of the world, from mere appearances that bear the mark of mortality and finitude, from transient, decaying things that "are and are not," while above lies the pure idea "that always is," unchanging and eternal, which is to say, divine.

But there is one problem. It is in fact *the* problem: Diotima, a woman,[1] is wise with the kind of knowing that corresponds to one of the most significant points of genuine Platonic teaching. Diotima speaks Plato's words: philosophy understood as Eros and cognitive ascent, as the contemplation of pure ideas through the desire for the eternally beautiful. There is thus no trace of misogyny here. Plato has indeed chosen a woman to teach his truth.

The presence of the female element is not only entrusted to Diotima as the protagonist of the Dialogue: in fact her speech as priestess is completely imbued with the theme and metaphor of pregnancy, parturition, parenting – bringing into the world. It is not by chance that Socrates functions as her pupil and reports her discourse: Socrates is an expert in the maieutic method, the art of the midwife who does not "insert" notions into the soul of the listener, but rather helps souls give birth to a truth that they already carry within them.

On the one hand, it seems that the feminine, understood as maternal experience, is an important element in Diotima's speech. But this element is so pervasive in the discourse that it goes beyond the degree necessary to indicate that it is a woman who is speaking. Femininity itself belongs structurally to Socrates' and Plato's philosophy. In other words, the works of Plato and Socrates seem marked by a *mimetic* desire for female experience. The pregnant, birth-giving male, like the male who practices midwifery, stands as the emblematic figure of true philosophy.

As a theatrical device, mimesis indeed dominates part of the *Symposium*. In its dramatic fiction the text consists of a series of speeches on Love given by various characters present at a feast at the house of Agathos. The characters appear on the "stage" one after the other, and address us "directly." Socrates happens to be among the characters, and we wait for his pronouncements on Love with lively expectation. Nevertheless, when it is his turn to speak, Socrates does not deliver his own speech but reports the words he had once heard spoken by Diotima. So Diotima is not an actual character in the *Symposium* – and whether or not such a person ever existed historically is quite another issue – but she becomes a character in this Dialogue who substitutes, as it were, for Socrates' own direct speech.[2] We could say then that when Socrates wants to give his own opinion on Love he chooses to speak through the mouth of a woman, a woman he claims to have known. Rather than reporting a famous speech, he chooses to present the discourse of this woman whom he designates as his teacher. Hence her words are words which he agrees with, and has appropriated as his own. Plato's device of dramatizing his philosophical discussions complicates things further, since, as we know, in most of the Dialogues, and certainly in the *Symposium*, it is Plato himself who is speaking to us through the voice of Socrates.

I am not interested in dealing here with the issue of the difference between the historical Socrates and the character of Socrates in Plato's Dialogues. Rather, I am concerned with emphasizing how the device of reported speech creates the mimetic effect of confusing or commingling the male and female voice. (Diotima is the only character who speaks while not being present at Agathos' banquet.) In other words, it is a woman who transmits the genuine teaching of Plato, and her words, far from being original or in some way rooted in the sex of the speaker, are the words of Plato re-echoing in a female voice.

We are still left with the question: why a female voice? Or rather, why a woman? Specific circumstances actually necessitated the theatrical device of reported speech. Plato could not have presented a woman speaking directly within the Dialogues because women were not admitted to the symposia. The exclusion of women from the venue dedicated to the exercise of philosophy is in fact ultimately emphasized in Plato's symbolism: Diotima is a *foreigner*, just like the servant from Thrace. Plato also designates that she is a priestess, meaning that she belongs to a sphere of knowledge where women are also allowed to speak.[3] This detail betrays a concern to bolster his choice of this character with additional justification. We must now investigate why Plato, in the midst of so many structural difficulties, explicitly wanted a woman to deliver the speech that was so important to him personally.

The question I already raised regarding Parmenides' goddess becomes an issue in Diotima's case also. What we find at work in both instances is a subtle and ambiguous strategy requiring that a female voice expound the philosophical discourse of a patriarchal order that excludes women, ultimately reinforcing the original matricide that disinvests them. But this symbolic strategy is even more significant in the case of Plato's Diotima, because here the symbolic matricide does not occur through the immediate dematerializing force of a blatantly abstract use of language, but rather through an evocative vocabulary based on the "mimesis of pregnancy." In Diotima's speech maternal power is annihilated by offering its language and vocabulary to the power that will triumph over it, and will build its foundations on annihilation itself.

Since love is the subject of the *Symposium*, human sexuality and sexual difference are explicitly thematized here. The issue of male homosexual love provides the principal framework for the thematic discussion of *both* sexes. This form of sexual practice was widespread among the Greeks, and was especially prevalent in Plato's circle, where it had the status of a kind of philosophical instruction. According to the conclusion of the Dialogue devoted to Diotima's speech, it is the love between two men that constitutes philosophy's erotic path, the route leading to the noetic attainment of the idea of the beautiful that constitutes the true exercise of philosophy. The non-philosophical, or rather anti-philosophical role of heterosexual love is thus clarified, since heterosexuality is articulated on the bipolar juxtaposition of bodily fertility (the reproduction of human children) with noetic fertility (the reproduction of divine discourses, the "children" of philosophers).

Aristophanes' disquisition on Love introduces the theme of the two human sexes into the dramatic unfolding of the Dialogue even before Socrates intervenes to report Diotima's teaching. It is Aristophanes who recounts an evocative myth that has become quite famous, and he tells his listeners how, at the beginning, the human race was divided into three sexes: male, female, and a third sex known as androgynous, that shared traits of the other two. The human shape was spherical. People had two faces, four arms, four legs, and two sets of genitals located at the front and back (*Symposium* 189d–190a; all unascribed references hereafter are to the *Symposium*). Therefore sexual identity could be described as double-male, double-female, and androgynous. But sexual intercourse did not take place between these primitive beings, because they "fathered and conceived, not in each other, but in the ground, like cicadas" (191c).

These early humans were nonetheless arrogant and over-bearing, and Zeus decided to humble them by cutting them in two "like people who slice eggs with a thread" (190d). He thus doubled their number, leaving each creature with two arms and legs, a single head, and a single set of genitals. What we see today is the result of this. Only two sexes – male and female – are considered to exist now, since the two halves of those ancient androgynous beings have been divided into the separate male and female components of their original, double-sexed identity. Love in fact originates from the dialectic of the original whole which was split in two. "Love collects the halves of our original nature, and tries to make a single thing out of the two parts so as to restore our natural condition" (191d). Each of us is therefore a half searching for our other half in order to recreate the lost whole, and when we think we have found it we grasp it, embracing and entwining ourselves with it.

This tendency toward fusion harks back to the three different wholes cut in half at the dawn of human origins, and it makes manifest three different kinds of sexual attraction: between male and male, female and female, male and female. It is attraction between male and female that tends to reconstitute the early androgynous human. Only this kind of attraction, known as heterosexual love, facilitates human regeneration (genesis) through

the union of male and female. In other words, only the kind of
sexual intercourse that originates from androgyny, and attempts
to recreate it, allows for the reproduction of the human species.

Despite its merit of assuring the continuation of the species,
Aristophanes unhesitatingly assigns a negative cast to heterosexual
love, since it is the result of a punishment meted out by Zeus.
Heterosexuality takes the place of reproduction "in the ground,"
in the manner of cicadas, which, apparently, was preferable
(as well as "predictable" since it is obvious that a double male
would give birth to another double male), and here we must
remember that the fruitfulness of male homosexual love is the
central thesis of the *Symposium*). The practice of heterosexual
love is indeed a "forced custom" (192b) for those who are born
with a homosexual nature and practice marriage out of sober
reproductive necessity. The descendants of androgynous beings,
however, tend to be inordinately adulterous. The scenario is quite
explicit, and it foreshadows an argument developed later by
Diotima: while necessary for the survival of the species, regeneration or the act of giving birth to human beings makes love a means
of carrying out the natural laws of reproduction. It is not an end
in itself. Hence the kind of love that is potentially procreative, the
kind of love that is inherited from androgynous beings, is reflected
pejoratively in the undignified image of heterosexual lovers. Indeed
heterosexuality consists of a practice of love the goal of which is
to be found elsewhere (in reproduction, in progeny). Homosexual
love, by contrast, does not produce anything other than or
external to itself, finding complete fulfillment within itself and
allowing the lovers to attend "to their work and . . . to the rest
of life" (191c).

In other words, love is not only separate from procreation,
but procreation itself is reduced to a biologically imposed social
function. In this way, the symbolic gain of separating love from
procreation is immediately translated into a negative or reductive
attitude toward procreation. Consequently, women's maternal
power becomes the physical means of carrying out sexed reproduction, which is understood as the fate imposed on humans as
a punishment from Zeus. Maternal power is so closely associated
with this negative view of human regeneration that it is totally

erased from the letter of the text. Clearly, it is implicitly regarded as a kind of natural apparatus that will lead mechanically to the accomplishment of human reproduction when activated by intercourse between men and women. The illogical absence of commentary on female homosexuality further emphasizes the misogynistic ramifications of the myth of origins. Female homo- sexuality is briefly mentioned as an amorous tendency arising from the original existence of double-female beings, but the remainder of the text is dedicated entirely to celebrating the educa- tional, political, and ethical advantages of love between men.

Aristophanes' account of the myth has the merit of emphasizing thematically the fundamental existence of a human species with two sexes, but it has the disadvantage of superimposing an inter- pretive logic that is intended to provide a theoretical basis for male homosexuality. This in turn translates into a general lack of interest in the love that women experience, and also implicitly denies the power of maternity. A symbolic matricide of the first degree has already been effected here. Significantly, the depreca- ting attitude that equates maternity with mere reproduction goes hand in hand with the kind of attitude that reductively attributes the very origin of life to a strategy imposed by the will of the punishing Zeus.

By the time it is Socrates' turn to speak the theoretical con- text of the argument has already been sketched out in its basic elements. There has been a clear statement on the lowly reproduc- tive function of heterosexual love and the higher value of male homosexual love. Diotima's words do not deal directly with the myth recounted by Aristophanes, but it serves as a preamble and implied frame for her speech.

As reported by Socrates, Diotima's speech defines Love principally as a "great daimon" (*Symposium* 202d), characterized by a kind of intermediacy between mortality and immortality, between the mortal and the divine. "Since it is in the middle it fills in between the two so that the whole is bound together by it" (202e). That is, Love unites the transient world to otherworldly eternity so that the philosopher learns how to rise from one to the other, thus finding his predestined home. It is precisely this quality of in-betweenness that makes Love a philosopher, since "his father was wise and resourceful, but his mother was not wise and lacked resources" (204b). He is neither all-knowing, since if he were he would not desire to know, nor completely ignorant, since if he were he would not aspire to something he does not know he needs. But the daimon Love indeed loves (*philei*) wisdom (*sophia*), just like philosophers. Love is lack and tension, desire and movement which never ceases nor finds fulfillment, since it is always in the middle, incapable of dissolving into nothingness or wholeness. Moreover, since Love was conceived on Aphrodite's birthday, it resembles the philosopher who loves what is beautiful, owing to the common tension between lack and fulfillment.

Love can therefore be found in every desire for beauty. It ultimately coincides with the desire for the good since, according to an axiom typical of Greek culture, each person can desire only what he or she considers his or her own good, given that it is absurd that one would wish evil for oneself. On the other hand – and here again a topos comes into play – there is no greater good than happiness. Diotima and Socrates thus agree on a basic definition: "love is wanting to possess the good forever" (206a) namely, it is the desire to be happy and to remain close to beauty.

Starting from this mutually acceptable definition, what now begins to be revealed in Diotima's speech is a vocabulary that springs from a mimesis of maternal imagery. Diotima specifies how love is in effect "a giving birth in beauty, both in body and in soul" (206b). This statement is crucial since the image of parturition is immediately presented side by side with the distinction between body and soul. Childbirth is evoked with the technical term *tokos*, which indicates giving birth, procreating, bringing a child into the world. The distinction between soul and body will enable philosophy to be defined as a birthing of the male soul and is linked to love between men.

Let us follow this argument in detail.

Mortal nature tries with every means to exist forever (*aei einai*, Parmenides' principle!), to achieve immortality. And this seems to become possible through the reproductive act, which always replaces an old person with a child. Clearly, this concerns the immortality of the species, rather than that of the individual. To be forever, *without change*, corresponds to the immortality of divine things that finds its true name in eternity. Earthly life is never eternal, but is by nature changing, transient, temporary. Transformation and decay are part of every individual, insofar as he/she never stays *the same*, *is* continuously *not*, and carries within the predestined *non-being* of death. These transformations correspond to the continuous change of scene wherein individuals replace each other on the stage of life. Indeed everyone dies, or will inevitably die, but others are born, to die in their own turn and to procreate others who will be born. Similarly, in the lives of individual persons, many of their parts decay, die, are born, transformed, and changed.

The immortality of the species lies therefore in its persistent capacity for change through the birth of the new, despite individual death. Giving birth through the body is thus the way in which "a mortal being participates in immortality" (208b). But, since mortals die, this sort of participation is merely symbolic. It is only the species that is perpetuated, managing to save itself from definitive *not-being*, from the annihilation of the human species, through the individual cycle of birth and death. The species is made up of individual lives characterized by frailty and destined to die. Precisely because of this, mortals generate another life that will endure beyond the death of the individual. The *strategy* through which a mortal being participates in immortality is seen as a kind of mechanism which enables the life of the species to be preserved through a regenerative cycle in which mortals themselves become the necessary vehicle of regeneration.

Here again death becomes the measure of birth, since birth is viewed and assessed from the perspective of death, as its concrete remedy. The binomial category mortal/immortal explicitly thematizes death. This is partly because humans are actually called mortals (meaning subject to death), according to an ancient lexical tradition. More importantly, however, the centralization of death allows the juxtaposition mortal/immortal to be rendered as individual/species, thus projecting the human gaze toward death, outward and onward, anxiously facing a voracious and unstoppable *future*. Evidently this does not resolve the anguish of individual death, which is nonetheless diffused and subsumed into the immortality of the species. Birth and regeneration thus become part of this mechanism, and are governed by it. According to the perspective that considers the body as split off from the soul, to be born is to come into the world to reproduce and to die, following the law of human self-preservation and therefore participating in the physical immortality of the species. This blind, cyclical pattern is based on a fear of death that embraces and sustains everything.[4]

As has often been confirmed, it is death, assumed as the measure of life, that lies at the bottom of this sort of reasoning. For men, the desire to be remembered and to "lay ... down immortal glory for eternal time" (208c) is an overwhelming one. Men love immortality – which is projected into the future through other people's memory – to the point that they will face any risk or hardship to win eternal fame. To achieve it, they are ready "even to die" (208d). The mention of death is emblematic in this context. Here again individual death is both the absolute symbol of a man's intolerable finitude, and something that he can take on in order to transcend and deny that very finitude. Though he cannot transcend death's insurmountable effect on individual life, he can at least negate its power to erase him forever from the world. Let at least remembrance endure, triumphing over the finitude imposed by death, even if death itself is the price of such victory!

The man who yearns above all others for immortal glory is the Homeric hero Odysseus. In the *Inferno*, Dante rightly chose to reward his hero with a memorable death. In Plato, however, the figure of Odysseus functions more particularly as a thematic opening to the discourse closest to his heart, the discussion on the conception and birth of the soul. Diotima distinguishes between two kinds of men. She points out that some are fertile mainly in their bodies, and hence "are more oriented toward women." These men participate in immortality through procreation. Other men are fertile mainly in their soul, since there are some things with which the soul can become pregnant and to which it can give birth (208e–209a).

It is hardly necessary for me to repeat that the language in this passage has a precise, strictly technical quality, and that similar usage can be traced elsewhere in Plato's work, revealing itself as a constant icon of philosophy (DuBois 1988: 169–83). The issue at stake is, quite literally, that of male maternity, and the art of midwifery practiced by Socrates fits neatly into this.[5] It is difficult to say that this discourse involves the simple deployment of a metaphor, because the metaphor ends up disempowering and negating the female experience – of motherhood as power – of which it is itself a metaphor. More precisely, the discourse could be described as a kind of mimesis. The result is an act of expropriation carried out through a woman's voice, namely the voice of someone against whom the expropriation is committed.

The mimesis is quite complete. It includes mating, conception, labor, parturition, and the newborn child. Its protagonist is homosexual love, which spurs men on to desire beautiful bodies and souls. Indeed when a man's soul is already fertile with such things as wisdom and justice, he seeks out the beautiful in order to give birth to these virtues. If he then meets a beautiful soul in a beautiful body, he attaches himself to the other man and "engages in many conversations with this man about virtue, about what a good man should be like, and what he should make it his business to do; thus he sets out to educate him" (*Symposium* 209c). In beauty and in love, the lovers thus finally give birth to and generate the things with which they were already pregnant, forever taking care of the offspring they have produced together. Because they have given birth to children who are more beautiful and more immortal, their union is certainly more intimate than the kind that produces children of flesh and blood (209c).

Examples of these beautiful and immortal offspring are seen in the poetry of Homer and the laws of Solon. Immortal progeny renders its creators immortal, or worthy of everlasting glory. "Many shrines have been dedicated to men because of this sort of children, but none at all because of their human offspring" (209e). Yet it is philosophy above all else that Diotima wishes to attribute to childbearing by homosexual lovers. What is envisioned here is a kind of amorous preparation for philosophizing, an erotic route toward higher knowledge.

The famous philosophical itinerary of love teaches the man who loves another man "to study beautiful things correctly and in their proper order," until the idea of beauty is attained, a beauty that is eternal: "it neither comes into being nor passes away, neither increases nor diminishes" (211a). The lover will gradually ascend from loving a single body to loving the beauty of all beautiful bodies. Finally, he will love the most precious beauty of souls, and above all the beauty of virtue and knowledge with which beautiful souls are filled. Through the infinite sea of beauty he will attain the contemplation of what has always been the true object of his unstoppable desire: beauty in itself, namely the idea of beauty to which philosophy aspires in its love of knowledge. Gradually ascending in successive stages toward the beautiful and the idea of beauty, love between men involves experiences such as mating, pregnancy, and giving birth to immortal discourses (namely philosophical discourses, the children of beautiful souls). On the other hand, it rises from the level of the body to the level of the soul, detaching itself from the transient to attain the eternal and the divine. In short, what emerges at this juncture is Diotima's initial distinction between body and soul, which was linked to her distinction between reproduction by heterosexual lovers (giving birth in beauty from the body) and the generation of philosophy that springs from homosexual love (giving birth in beauty from the soul). But the distinction is now reconfigured to indicate an internal division within the erotic route toward wisdom. In fact, love among men involves associating with other men's bodies. It involves the knowledge and desire of their physical beauty. However, it neither stops there nor causes the reproduction of other bodies. On the contrary, it moves "in ascending steps" (211b) toward beauty in itself. This kind of beauty shines through those bodies, and yet, precisely for this reason, it is something quite different from the body's fleeting and transient appearance. In this way the body is once again linked to the experience of love, but only as the first step, as an immediate and easy entry to a realm that is not at all corporeal and is actually endowed with the traits of eternity that mortal bodies tragically lack.

Thus death always determines the categories of discourse, describing on the one hand a bodily life that is marked by transience, and on the other hand a life of the mind capable of dwelling with the eternal. Because the idea of beauty is eternal, "neither comes into being nor passes away, neither increases nor diminishes" (211a), this is also true of the philosophical discourses to which the soul gives birth in its presence. They are far more immortal than Homer's poetry and Solon's laws, which have been carried down by memory and tradition, because in philosophical discourses the eternal itself – the eternity of pure ideas – is close to the human thought that contemplates and absorbs it. This constitutes true thought, which as such partakes of the eternity of that which is true, and finds its home there.

If a breath of eternity touches human bodies, it is the beauty that arises from the idea of the beautiful like a shining, ephemeral trace, since bodies grow old and die, and the bodies that mate with each other in heterosexual union generate other bodies which are destined to die. These are fleeting individual instances of the kind of immortality that the species earns for itself through its necessary, monotonous cycle of births and deaths.

The male soul can give birth to offspring of a very different kind, which cannot be overtaken by death. This immortal, even eternal progeny cannot be consumed by any kind of cyclic process.

According to Page DuBois, the psychoanalytical model of phallocentricity and castration is especially rooted in the "post-Platonic metaphysical representation of woman that sees her as a defective male – the female is the male, but lacking" (1988: 30), which is to say "lacking" the penis. Hence the famous psycho-analytical category of "penis envy" which is supposed to plague the female unconscious. Indeed, the patriarchal order was already firmly in place at the time, and the phallus had already claimed its symbolic position of command. But Plato's position seems transitional, since it does not emphasize the figure of woman as a castrated male, and almost suggests the opposite, namely a sort of "womb envy" which manifests itself in the masculine mimesis of maternity, with obvious complications resulting from the matricidal, patriarchal context.

The text of the *Symposium* is indeed exemplary of this kind of operation. Mimesis is not simply evident here; indeed it is explicitly sought after in the technical quality of the language. More importantly, however, what is actually established by this mimetic operation is the symbolic patriarchal order emblematized by the phallic. It is not that phallocracy suddenly springs to the fore, to use a simple and obvious image: phallic symbolism had already been rooted for some time in Greek culture (Keuls 1985), and it functions as an implicit background to Plato's argument. Yet here indeed something deeper is given expression, something more ancient, which both establishes phallocratic rituals and makes them possible. To stay within the language of psychoanalysis, the motivating force is the lack of and the envy of maternal power that men do not possess. It is procreation as the female experience denied to men.

At this juncture in Plato's writing the stakes stand out with particular force, and enable us to read the complex symbolic fabric into which they are woven. Above all, we see the binomial birth/death linked again to the opposition feminine/masculine, and this link is significant. These are the double threads of the web, but they weave a pattern where the male thread of death knots itself around the female thread, forcing it into intricate designs, which are both obfuscating and mimetic. Thus, the symbolic force of the repressed pole is taken up through a mimetic disguise, so that maternal power, having been torn away from its roots in the context of birth, cloaks the matricidal cultivators of death with its symbolic power; and in this way birth, as the original locus of maternal power, is ultimately negated. It is turned into something else – either mere reproductive function, or a way of designating the unbelievable nothingness from which we come.

According to a well-known ritual practice, the lion slayer decorates himself with the slain animal's skin, imitating its movements and appropriating its terrifying manner. This mimetic performance suggests envy as well as its expiation. However, we are certainly not dealing with something as simple as a lion hunt in Plato's text. The motive at work here is not the difference between human and animal power, but the kind of sexual difference within the human species itself that distributes power in an uneven way to the male and female sex, since, *kata physin*, the act of bringing both sexes into the world, is conceded only to the female. Indeed the primary locus and precondition of all other power is found in the Great Mother, from whom every man and woman originates by nature and by birth, since in order to be good, rich, noble, honored, and beautiful one must at least *be there*. One must be living, one must have already been born.[6]

The natural imbalance of power between the two sexes (an imbalance that is certainly a literal fact) eventually brings about a scenario where envy becomes possible, and is actually activated. It is hardly surprising then that the envy males feel for females explicitly negates the natural/natal order where the imbalance of power is really rooted. Nor is it surprising that this negation is motivated by the elementary logic underlying the juxtaposition of birth and death, since death takes away the power to live that birth bestows. Death removes this power in every case and at all times, since it comes to every man and woman, and is not necessarily something inflicted by one person on another. Even though the earliest text in Western culture is an emblematic narration of a war and therefore an account of death inflicted by and suffered by men, it is not death at the hands of an armed murderer that this culture nurtures and supports, but death in itself – the fact of being mortal. Nevertheless, it follows that a death which is inflicted or risked at war (death at the hands of men) becomes symptomatically in this text the arena in which male valor can be measured.

So death as such becomes the center of the patriarchal order that is as determined to establish its meaning on the power of death as it is increasingly anxious of this fearful power that designates an end, rather than a beginning. This annihilating force consists solely in depriving the living of the power to live, especially depriving those who have decided to deny the maternal power that has brought them to life. Thus the centralization of death forces matricidal men to play death's own card of self-annihilation. This is the annihilation of nothingness, the Parmenidean insistence that nothingness cannot be, so that everlasting being can be a remedy for the nothingness of death which had been placed at the center, owing to its promises of immense power.

Consequently, the tendency to measure the meaning of one's own life on the fact that we must leave life through death, rather than the fact that we enter it through birth, and the desire for immortality are one and the same. Metaphysics progresses logically along its preordained path, a path where the denial of birth and infinite duration are obsessively conjoined. The unbearability of impermanence is imaged in death, and is ultimately transferred to birth. Thus birth is found guilty of generating bodies subject to death. In the meantime, a distinct philosophical thought – which is undying but nonetheless dissatisfied with mere immortality – claims access to the eternal, without any birth whatever.

Thus the interplay of immortality and eternity, or, in Platonic language, the interplay of a noetic soul and the ideas that constitute its objects, enacts a necessity that the soul discovers within itself, transferring the ideas it already has into discourse. This eternal is already the soul's substance and home, so that the vicissitudes of the body are located in an *elsewhere* that is a prison, an accident. The mimesis of maternal power is acted out here, since the operation is seen as a giving birth through discourse to something that the noetic soul carries within it. In philosophical discourse spoken by men, the act of engendering something that is not subject to being engendered (because it is eternal) indeed partakes of human life. It is a sort of *genesis* freed from transience, since here, paradoxically, the nature of the philosophical child is *ageneton*, "not born," insofar as it exists from the beginning of time and forever.

In Plato this mimesis is both subtle and crude. Its subtlety lies in its function of sublimating envy by allowing men to appropriate the reality of birth, extracting it from the sexed territory of the feminine where it is rooted by nature. It is crude because, as the philosopher gets carried away by the act of mimesis, he spares us neither homosexual mating, conception, gestation, nor labor pains.

It must be said that in both its subtle and crude aspects, Platonic mimesis is emblematically manifest in the dialogue's explicitly technical language. Nonetheless, it remains an isolated document in the Western philosophical tradition. Post-Platonic thought would in fact prescribe the mere act of looking as a remedy for male envy. No longer seen in its internal/secret power to generate, the female body becomes something that displays itself on the outside as deprived of the phallic appendage. Plato's text is so much more significant for the fact that it belongs to the beginnings of philosophy, to the dawn of an age of envy whose results were about to be consolidated into a system and which still revealed the matricidal expropriation that sustains them. Besides, traces of the technical language pertaining to conception and motherhood persist in the tradition. But what remains with us above all is the masculine homosexual quality that characterizes the places, forms, and contents of knowledge, even though empirically practiced homosexual love has become clandestine.

In this regard, it is not difficult to find someone ready to concede that in the West knowledge is organized as a sort of "masculine club" from which women are excluded, as has been the case with politics. However, this admission is rarely followed by the awareness that the sign of masculinity not only affects the actual presence of men and their relative privileges, but its intimate essence energizes the practices and contents of knowledge. The male homosexual route through which knowledge is generated, which was sketched out by Plato in a few crude strokes, is in itself an enduring mark of the Western tradition. This tradition bears witness to the fact that men are united by love and esteem for their own sex, and can thus produce a symbolic order that perpetuates a kind of autistic self-absorption originating in their ancient envy of maternal power. In short, with the power of matricidal knowledge, they give birth to themselves. They come into a world structured by logocentric power where to be born and to live are, not without reason, the object of a merely reproductive function regulated by politics.

Man generates man, as Aristotle used to say when he wished to attribute the causality of procreation entirely to the father's sperm. But it is more correct to say that men generate Man, thus giving birth as they had planned to something eternal and universal, at least in its pretensions. Men are necessarily finite. They die, but their neutral/masculine essence endures, eternalized in Western culture.

The self-governing imaginary of the Greek male is very ancient, as is evident from the earliest literary texts. In Hesiod we find the description of a human race consisting only of men, until Pandora, the first woman, came to join them as a punitive gift from the gods. The female "womb" appears with Pandora's "box" from which all evils flow, as offspring flows from women's wombs. For the offspring, genesis is a *becoming*, whose end point is the extreme evil of death. But this race, consisting only of men, indicates the not-yet of birth and therefore the mournful becoming generated by the "box" of a woman's body. In Hesiod's work we also find a supreme expression of maternal power in the divine figure of Gaia, the Earth. At a very early time, she generated Uranus, or the Heavens, on her own, only to be "covered" by him in an uninterrupted sexual embrace that supposedly prevented other children from emerging from the mother's womb.

Therefore, in Hesiod's imaginary we already find the representation of both the feminine and the masculine as self-sufficient, in a sort of open contradiction or unresolved ambiguity. The feminine is a parthenogenesis of divine imprint, typical of the figure of the Great Mother. The masculine, of human imprint, suggests the presence of a human race composed only of men, which women join later, bringing with them the capacity to bear children that pertains to them. The figure of Zeus giving birth seems obliquely related to both.

In fact, the Zeus of mythical tradition stages a mimesis of maternity which is completely explicit and "concrete," since he gives birth to his daughter Athena from his skull. She is already an adult, bedecked with shining weaponry. He also gives birth to his infant son Dionysus from his thigh. The second birth is particularly interesting, because its symbolic underpinnings are pervaded with envy / appropriation of maternal power, and overshadowed by the preventive matricide of Semele, the woman whom Zeus impregnated with the future Dionysus. In fact, having mated with the mortal Semele, and having made her pregnant with Dionysus, Zeus immediately strikes her to death with his lightning. Then he snatches away the unborn child and puts it in his thigh to allow it to grow and develop. Hence, after the proper period of gestation within the god's thigh, Dionysus is born from the paternal body. In this case, matricide and the masculine mimesis of maternity are linked in a very manifest way and with such transparent logic as to need no further comment. The symbolic weight of this link is too triumphant and simplistic to be definitive, and it bears down upon the extraordinary "identity" of the son born to him: the divine Dionysus.

Born of a father who killed his mother, Dionysus is a divine figure always surrounded by women. Significantly, this privileged relationship with the female element becomes indispensable for one not born of woman. As an infant, Dionysus was raised by Semele's sisters, and was nursed by the Nymphs and other women. These groups of sisterly women worked together, and were perpetually tormented by the enemies of the divine infant because of their tender care. Even when Dionysus becomes an adult, women (the Maenads or the Bacchae) preside over his cult, reaching him directly through delirium and possession. The "twice born" god thus seems to carry within him the feminine imprint of his originally denied birth, and seems to embody his gender with a certain ambiguity. He is sometimes called *arsenothelus* (hermaphrodite), and, according to one version of the myth, was raised as a girl (Otto 1965: 176).

The best-known element linked to this widespread, age-old cult is the relationship between Dionysus and the Bacchae, which mirrors the archetypal relationship between Dionysus and women following a constant pattern. Often delirious or running away, these women always appear in sisterly clusters. In fact, the Bacchae represent recklessness and delirium as a radically transgressive behavior with respect to women's domestic, wifely role. It is a self-induced derangement that upsets the established order, rather than the kind of unbridled sexual behavior usually attributed to the satyrs in their drunken Dionysian frenzy, which is how people have mistakenly viewed it. It is a kind of infringement of the normal laws of the social order, a sort of divine madness, where the primal and instinctual element seems to spring from repressed separations, and overtakes the societal codes that prescribe a domestic, maternal role for women.

As Euripides recounts, the Bacchae "left their looms and shuttles." Swept up by frenzy and inebriated with the god, they ran through wildernesses, and with a touch of their hands drew milk, wine, and honey from the earth (see also Plato, *Ion* 534a).

They tamed raging bulls, while snakes with quivering tongues licked their cheeks. And "mothers ... abandoned babies; their breasts gorged with milk, they held wolf cubs in their arms, or young gazelles, and were suckling them" (Euripides, *Bacchae* 695ff). This kind of behavior is crucial to the characterization of the Bacchae, given that "the picture of the maenad who gives suck to a beast of prey appears often in works of art" (Otto 1965: 102).

We find in Dionysian women an extraordinary, divine movement that marks them off from the domestic role. This movement does not constitute an arbitrary sort of transgression, but leads in a specific direction, that is, toward the animal realm to which the human element is conjoined *through* the feminine. This is not new. On the contrary, a recurrent cultural topos has long linked woman with the animal element, as though her humanity were intimately imbued with it. We have only to think of the Sphinx, the Sirens, and Pandora's body painted with animal images. The conventional interpretation of the link is very simple: in the ontologically descending hierarchy god–man–animal it is the spiritual element, or thought, that unites man with god, while the bodily element unites him with animals. It is therefore obvious that woman – consisting wholly of the despised element of embodiedness that links humankind with the animal realm – figuratively reveals a hybrid constitution. In short, a feminine pole represented as almost-bestial or less-than-human corresponds to a masculine pole which represents itself as almost-divine or more-than-human.

The myth of Dionysus can also be interpreted in this fashion. High culture suggests that what is at stake here is a deep symbolic truth concerning the link between woman and the animal realm. This "positive" truth is supposedly unhinged from the traditional hierarchy that has the noetic/divine element at its highest point. On the other hand, however, this link explicitly leads back to the figure of maternity as a place where the animal element is revealed as divine, in a sort of reversed hierarchy. So the figural hybrid woman/animal is represented as a peculiar bond between the maternal and the animal realm. (And yet its man/animal variant reveals the complexity of its hermeneutical codes.) Indeed the symbolic core lies in a kind of dramatic substitution of the animal child for the human child. In one of its crudest versions the myth tells of how the daughters of Minia, carried away by Dionysian delirium, tore apart one of their own young, adding to infanticide the kind of maternal behavior seen in wild animals.

In addition to human sacrifice and the cannibalistic ritual that the very figure of Dionysus evokes, what we find here is the repetition of a symbolic trajectory directed away from the present and toward the past, from socially codified normalcy toward an unimaginable origin, from the human toward the animal realm. This happens precisely by way of the feminine/maternal. Indeed the shift from dwellings to the wild, from the city to the wilderness, from socially codified human motherhood to unbridled bestial maternity, is manifest here. That this shift should happen in madness, in dementia or delirium only makes its backward movement stronger; a movement from the specifically human equation between *logos* and socialized living back to *a-logia*. Therefore the logical quality of the mind is lost, abandoned, for the sake of attaining something that precedes it, namely, a primal animal memory that humans (not without reason known as "animals capable of *logos*") carry with them as that from whence they came.

I believe that the necessity of transmitting the animal element through the female line is rooted in the idea of an original animality, and women can stir this memory.[7] In fact, the threshold between the animal and the human realm leaps to our eyes when viewed from a perspective that regards birth as the wellspring of human life through a maternal *continuum* that stretches back in time in an infinite succession of mothers. In a distant time – the indeterminable *past* of humankind – the link between the two realms has imperceptibly erased its own foundation in the maternal *continuum*. In post-Darwinian terms, it is difficult to determine whether this link is articulated in the shift of primates from simians to humans that happened over millions of years.[8] It is certain that this passage happened through innumerable sequence of births from female bodies. In the brief time of several millennia, the transmission of life has seen an unpredictable consolidation and deployment of new forms up to the definitive human form. The link in this transmission has certainly been feminine, perhaps precisely the vehicle of embodied experience that surfaces in the delirium of the Bacchae as "the frenzied, all-engulfing torrent of life which wells up from the [maternal] depths that gave it birth" (Otto 1965: 95).

What we find here is a radical shift in our way of looking at human origins, creating a perspective directed toward birth. This new way of looking allows us to see the female human creature and, behind her and through her, a genetic prehistory of animal origin that is actually felt and stored in the memory of the flesh.[9] In short, the Maenads lead our gaze toward the past, immersing themselves in it also. This is so because the origin always happens first and lies behind and before everything, and because the past of living humans is an infinite procession of births in reverse. In it, maternal power, which links this chain of births into infinity, is shot through with the innocent transformation of the human into the animal realm, and of the latter into something else, and so on, again and again. To all of this we give the indefinite name of earth, understood as feminine. It has no beginning and therefore no nothingness,[10] since the beginning has always initiated, generating both backward and toward infinity, within the horizon (adequate to the observer) that contains it and continues to be repeated and confirmed every time a woman gives birth.

Many symbolic intersections are concentrated in the polyvalent material of Dionysian myth. They are structured around a central theme of birth, played out mainly on the retributive correspondence between an act of matricide (Semele's death by lightning) and the furious return of the mothers (the Bacchae). Hence we have not only a strikingly mimetic birth from the matricidal father, but also the mothers' collective reappropriation of the scene. The women stage a deployment of prehuman, infinite maternal power, indicating that the divine does not reside in the hierarchical end point of the process of humanization (in the anthropomorphic deities or in the god of pure thought), but at the earliest point, at the origin, in the animal innocence that holds onto life without reflection.

In Nietzschean terms, we find Apollo and Dionysus at the end point, a masculine god produced by the mind, and a feminine god preserved in the memory of the infinite, immemorial beginning. But he is still a male god. What the presence of the god reveals is the animal element as a locus of the divine, causing havoc in the ascending hierarchy animal–man–god, and hardly by chance. On the one hand, this hierarchy posits man at the center of the link between the "lower" animal element and the "higher" divine element. On the other, it repeats this pattern by separating the material from the spiritual principle in man himself, body from thought, and so on. On the contrary, here the divine within the animal element suggests an immediate and innocent adherence to life where *logos* functions both as a specific principle of humanization and as a loss and distance from its divine origin. It is divine because it lives in perfection without knowing itself to live. Or, more exactly, without knowing what it is.

In fact, Dionysus is often indicated as a god of birth and death, and therefore, ultimately, as a god of the primal flow of life where birth and death are but rhythm and cadence. The centrality of the female figures that surround him at this point facilitates the symbolic expression of a kind of death that is not yet placed in isolation at the center, as though dismally supporting the obsession with metaphysics, but is linked to birth as to a living context of its own occurring. In short, this kind of death does not provide the measure of life's meaning, but is measured by life, in the everlasting range of a birth process that has always generated and will always be renewed.

Besides, the myth's narrative sequence clearly displays a process of "depersonalization." In fact we move beyond individual figures, such as Semele, Zeus, and Dionysus, to figural clusters consisting of groups of sisters and crowds of women. In other words, there is a symbolic passage from the specific motherhood of individual women (though negated and denied) to motherhood in general, understood as a feminine link to the divine animal element of origin. The process of "depersonalizing" the individual figure (while conserving its gendered foundation) thus seems to have the function of bringing life itself to the fore as a primitive and "prelogical" phenomenon to which all those living and of woman born really belong. The result is that individual death in its dramatic, centripetal meaning is immediately relegated to the background, as something that in the larger scheme of things belongs to the primitive phenomenon of life.

From this perspective, it is not without reason that our disinvestment from death ultimately abolishes the centrality of nothingness, since there is no nothingness in the incessant and internal labor of life's metamorphoses. There can be no nothingness if living human creatures turn their eyes away from their end, and look instead toward the infinite, embodied origin from whence they come. Indeed, if the nothingness of death, this sinking into nothingness through death, makes any sense, it does so for the dying person. At the moment of death, one's singularity ceases to consist of the form of life organized in a unified way that constitutes the self. In fact, from the point of view of infinite living matter, one's own death is a metamorphosis that one expects. The nothingness of death must be linked to the self-reflexive logocentric consciousness of humans, since animals seem to adhere innocently to the ritualistic changes of life, managing to leave the world with the quiet bewilderment of creatures unaware of living their own death.

What I am trying to suggest is that the mythic context that surrounds the figure of Dionysus bears visible traces of a symbolic web which is held in place by birth. This suggests that maternal power is the necessary site of the link with our boundless pre-human origins. Precisely because of this, it opens up a conceptual trajectory that moves from living individuals to life itself, rather than from individuals to their own death. In this framework we obviously find the categories of death, birth, life. But also, especially, we find the categories of animal, human, and divine. Here, however, these categories seem scattered into an anomalous and disheveled pattern, in contrast to the tradition that developed upon other (overturned) hierarchies.

In her book *A Paixão segundo G.H.* (*The Passion according to G.H.*), Clarice Lispector recounts a process of depersonalization that allows her to rediscover an innocent sense of belonging to "the forbidden weft of life" (1988: 7).[11] The protagonist is a wealthy middle-class woman, whom we know only by her initials G.H. She lives a sort of mystical experience, the adventure of a soul, in the enclosed space of her room, and happens to experience the "absence" of the self that allows divine, primeval life to emerge. "I was about to face within myself the degree of living so originary that it bordered on the inanimate" (1988: 15). G.H. abandons "humanized" life, namely the personal identity consisting of the unified organization of meaning that inserts her into a codified system where she has a face, a name, a role, a secondary social position as a woman. In so doing, she unexpectedly encounters the forms of a "profound disorganization" (1988: 3). These are life's multifarious inarticulateness, simultaneous immediacy, and "matter [that] resonates with attention, resonates with process, resonates with inherent nowness" (1988: 132). Lispector also calls this "the neutral," meaning the absence or, better still, the indifference within absence of "human organization," wherein the individuality of each person consists. This individuality is a kind of isolation, a separateness from the other, a reference back to the self. In the "neutral," every self, every "I," expresses indifferently the ritualism of an impersonal life consuming its infinite forms. It is this life of inhuman forms into which the dying person is transformed that prompted Clarice's fearful premonition of the long exposure of her corpse to other people's eyes, creating a sort of wanton spectacle of the metamorphic appearances of life active even in death.[12]

In fact, from this dehumanized perspective, death is but an event experienced by the living individual in his or her passage toward infinite, impersonal life, just as Clarice herself testifies in the quiet words that precede her death by a few hours. "I will be an impalpable substance without even a single trace of memory of last year" (cited in Morino 1982: 167–8). There is therefore a sort of contrasting perspective between the singularity of the living individual, who experiences his or her own death as a definitive threshold to the irreparable, and therefore as his or her nothingness, and the infinite life that lives on from this individual death and from a thousand deaths in "tranquil rawness" and an "advanced, profound, perfumed decay" (Lispector 1984: 43). This infinite life is indeed untouched by nothingness, since it is the boundless space of metamorphous appearances. Nothingness, like a sudden darkness in the eyes of the dying, can indeed be felt in this contrasting perspective, given that the moment of death is the simultaneous intersection, and hence the annihilation, of the contrast itself: "I don't know what it's like, because I'm not dead yet, and when I'm dead I won't know it either. Who knows, maybe death is not so dark after all. Maybe it is dazzlingly bright."

Clearly, the issue here is not darkness or light, since both dazzling light and darkness blind the eyes, and since this definitive blindness of the individual is our own inability to see, hear, and know, which we call death. The problem is rather that the configuration of nothingness has been completely entrusted to the partiality of the human individual, aspiring to omnipotence and experiencing the crucial moment of its actualization. The life of the "dirty, perishable" world, on the other hand, that vibrant, infinite life which is full, yet innocent, of a "deep murder," remains a space untouched by nothingness, which the individual is allowed to observe, if at all, with loving revulsion, or with dizzy attachment to a "silent, slow, insistent" reality of a perhaps horrible yet boundless appearance (1984: 44).

In this way nothingness, as the no-more of the self's individuality from the perspective of the dying, is ultimately conquered by the unending metamorphosis of impersonal life. Precisely from that life that already was at the beginning of every living human – and even before the beginning – and which everyone embodies for the span of an individual existence, as of mother born.

There is a crucial, difficult passage about this in *The Passion according to G.H.* The journey that enables the female protagonist to see and savor "a prehuman divine life" (Lispector 1988: 93) takes place in her comfortable middle-class apartment, reaching a climax in the vision of a black cockroach that she crushes between the doors of her wardrobe. In the banality of everyday experience, which constitutes the setting, the crucial figure to the passage toward the divine "vital element linking things" (1988: 92) is thus an animal, a disgusting insect, a cockroach. Yet the effectiveness of the insect as a vehicle for divine epiphany is not diminished. It serves a similar function to that of the Bacchae's wild beasts, and it has a similar meaning. For Lispector, the cockroach represents the spontaneity of an animal's experience of life, an existence without consciousness, love, suffering. She writes: "Its only differentiation in life is that it has to be either male or female. I had been thinking of it only as female since whatever is caved in at the middle must be female" (1988: 85). As the text progresses, the importance of the female gender attributed to the cockroach becomes more and more manifest, since pregnancy and motherhood are openly indicated as the crucial point where individual life is generated via the feminine from impersonal life, from the neutrality that sustains and surpasses it. Indeed the narration stylistically shifts into direct speech addressed to the mother, where the repeated invocation "Mother" marks the writer's words as those of a *daughter* to her mother.

We thus find in the *daughter's* thoughts a thematic focus on death and birth that is surprisingly derived from the Greek litany of "coming and going into nothingness." It pursues a radical path that undoes the centrality of the omnipotent, disembodied "I" built on the metaphysics of nothingness. In fact, Lispector descends into the neutral area of impersonal life not simply to rediscover the nullification of the "I," but also to find that sexed maternal root that links every "I" to impersonal life itself, every living being to his or her beginning in an origin that has innocently generated every beginning for all time. Precisely what is "crushed in life is female," for every living individual comes from a mother and consequently every woman contains the continuum of her past and future within her present: "her fifteen million daughters, from that time down to myself" (1988: 57). This maternal continuum is the locus of human regeneration according to the ritual of life that is never born and never dies, but is deployed *ad infinitum* in the birth and death of individual existences.

The theoretical trajectory and its structural categories seem to offer a storehouse of the traces of a female symbolic order which the Dionysian myth allows us to glimpse without much resistance. Starting in the "here and now," as is necessary and inevitable, from the standpoint of the individual living human, I would describe the central axis of this order more precisely as a looking back toward the past: toward a root that bears the sign of its origin, rather than forward, anticipating, planning, and projecting limits, as well as the obsession with transcending the individuality of mortal life. As Lispector also testifies, it is indeed evident that the backward gaze of the human individual encounters first of all his or her own birth in the figure of a mother who brought him/her into the world. Female sexual difference, in its aim of recovering meaning, becomes visible here, in such a way as to prevent universal/neutral Man from finding a meaningful space on the stage in any important scene. Pursuing this perspective, apart from the undeniable visibility of sexual difference, the mother is in many ways a *threshold* between the full and irreducible concreteness of each and every living person and the world from which individuals come and are shaped: a world which already exists, before, and even despite, their individuality.

It is indeed in many ways a threshold, because on the one hand the mother is the threshold between myself, as I find myself already here as a daughter, and the whole world, where without my mother I could never have been. This observation makes sense if it denotes finitude, contingency, and fortuity. But it is gratuitous if the point is to highlight the dread of nothingness, the frightening possibility of my nothingness in the fortuitousness of my being (a being). The theoretical possibility of not being here at all, of not having been born, is not at all frightening when contemplated from my concrete sense of being my mother's daughter, even though it seems to provide a morbid fascination to romantic minds. In this case, it is precisely the fortuitous element that sparks our curiosity and draws the gaze backward toward the infinite chain of mothers. Each one forms a link in a sequence of births that might not have existed or might have existed otherwise. Each one is therefore a pawn in the game of every woman's fate, including mine – my being present, with all the concrete fortuitousness that this implies; this body, sex, face, place, time, biography.[13] In this way, the mother also becomes the threshold in a game that everyone plays because it has already been played with them, as men and women. But here it is maternal power that makes the rules: by interrupting the game, as is the case with Demeter, or by deciding when she would like it to take place. (Pregnant women often find amusement in secretly imagining the sex and the features of their unborn child, as well as the events of its future.)

In another way, the mother is also the link that leads from the individual to the "impersonal," to the infinite life described by

Lispector, of which the "I" constitutes a temporary form. The mother's identity as a threshold becomes more complex in this case, since every mother is a conduit for the vibrant process of pure life and the undeniable living individuality of those born from her. Furthermore, through "the fifteen million daughters" who precede her, she is the link within the human species to infinite life, carrying the embodied memory of the human and prehuman within her. As Lispector says, at the time when the fifteen million daughters, of whom she herself is a daughter, signal to her the absolute importance of her sex: "I had always been in life, it mattered little that it was not I properly speaking, not the thing that I customarily call 'I.' I have always been in life" (1988: 57).

This embodied memory goes back to the prehuman through an infinite progression. Within this maternal memory, the animal realm becomes a symbol linked to the female, as well as a feminine expression of the divine. Here, "animal" does not necessarily connote a panther or a bull. It might merely indicate a cockroach, or could even mean "a protoplasm or a protein" rather than an animal (1988: 94). And yet the animal is closer to it, not only in evolutionary terms, but above all in a resemblance that makes it a living singularity, individually organized, that nevertheless adheres to life with unselfconscious innocence. To quote Lispector again: "I felt that animals were still one of the things close to God, a matter that has not yet invented itself, which is still warm from birth, and at the same time something that immediately stands on its feet, is thoroughly alive, that lives fully every instant, never a little at a time, that never spares itself, that never wears itself out completely" (Lispector 1960: 121).

The symbolic valence most clearly offered to the gaze – even though most hidden within this maternal, female link to animality – is perhaps precisely that of a painless conciliation between individuality and infinite life. It is the sense of belonging to an individual existence which "lives every instant to the full," but which for this very reason must not *know it*. For humans (animals equipped with logos) the problem is evidently unresolvable. Nonetheless, in the embrace of our infinite origin, Western philosophy can mark an abrupt shift of its famous destiny. Indeed the god who loves to be called "thought of thoughts" disappears irremediably in the face of the kind of divinity that splendidly knows nothing about self or other, and lives simply because it has been born.

Nonetheless, when at the final, most recent hour – having, for unfathomable reasons woven her way up to human logos via the feminine – it is her turn to *know*, then perhaps this female deity will demand that the splendor of her origins find grateful, knowing names in her daughters' speech.

Notes

Foreword

1 See Sandra Kemp and Paola Bono (eds) *Italian Feminist Thought* (Oxford; Oxford University Press, 1991) and *The Lonely Mirror* (Oxford: Blackwell, 1992); see also Cavarero's contribution in Gisela Brock and Susan James (eds) *Beyond Equality and Difference: citizenship, feminist politics, and female subjectivity* (London and New York, Routledge, 1992).

2 For an introduction to the line run by this group, see Milan Women's Bookshop, *Sexual Difference: a theory of social symbolic practice* (Bloomington: Indiana University Press, 1990).

3 For an interesting introduction, regrettably available only in Italian, of the work of this group, see Il Filo di Arianna (ed.), *La differenza non sia un fiore di serra* (Milan: Franco Angeli, 1991).

4 For the proceeding of this conference see C. Marcuzzo and Anna Rossi-Doria, *La ricerca delle donne: studi femministi in Italia* (Turin: Rosenberg & Sellier, 1987).

5 A. Cavarero, "Per una teoria della differenza sessuale," in Diotima, *Il pensiero della differenza sessuale* (Milan: La Tartaruga, 1987), pp. 43–79.

6 A. Cavarero, "Dire la nascita," in Diotima, *Mettere al mondo il*

mondo (Milan: La Tartaruga, 1990), pp. 93–122.

7 Giuliana Bruno, *Streetwalking on a Ruined Map: cultural theory and the city films of Elvira Notari* (Princeton: Princeton University Press, 1993).

8 This expression is suggested as a figuration for the postmodern condition by Maurizia Boscaglia in "Unaccompanied ladies: feminist, Italian and in the Academy," *differences*, 2/3 (1991), pp. 122–35.

9 For an interesting assessment of the Italian situation in a comparative international context, see Paola Bono (ed.), *Ouestioni di teoria femminista* (Milan: La Tartaruga, 1993); see also Ida Dominijanni's article in *The European Journal of Women's Studies*, 1/1 (1994).

10 See the important contribution by Teresa de Lauretis, "The essence of the triangle; or, taking the risk of essentialism seriously," *differences*, 1/2 (1988), pp. 3–37.

Chapter 1   Penelope

1 Homer's interpreters have not failed to observe how "strange" it is that Penelope does not recognize her spouse, especially given the fact that those who love him do recognize him. Some commentators have also added that this strangeness might indicate a poorly concealed infidelity on Penelope's part (cf. Devereux, 1982: 259–69). I think, however, that this strangeness actually indicates a different hermeneutical order, according to which Penelope manifests her estrangement and keeps herself estranged from the logic of Odysseus' "great story" narrated in the *Odyssey*.

2 It is not my intention here to attribute the valence of "repetitive" to feminine *metis* as such. In my theft, Penelope (like the other figures) is only a single piece in the mosaic of a potential female symbolic order. Obviously, this order does not take a definitive shape in my text. In other words, the female symbolic order is not found in its entirety in Penelope. Only some of it is present: a sign, an aspect, a moment. We find, for example, the figural representation of *separatism* as a political practice that favors women's rhythms and spaces. We also find the sense of estrangement from patriarchal codes that is manifest in these spaces. And we find the conquest of a kind of self-belonging, rooted in the company of other women within a shared space. In short, we find a figural representation of some of the terms that constitute a female political vocabulary. This new terminology is not concerned with giving an impression of unity.

It does not hesitate to enlarge a fragment to the point of seeming excessive. In Penelope's *metis*, it is the valence of her repetitive gesture that constitutes excess. But this confirms that the valence alludes to a kind of intelligence inseparable from the body, if related to its setting. What is more, it alludes to the intelligence of everyday experience, constantly mindful of the need to create a sense of roots and space.

3 Here I begin the labor of my analytical reading of philosophical texts, which I will also impose on my female readers. I could not spare them this, for the difficult context from which I freely steal these female figures is neither innocent nor indifferent to my theft. The original context precludes and conceals the possibility that female figures can rise to express a symbolic order of their own. But it does not do this in a simple way (say, with the basic erasure of women as subjects of discourse). It does so by constructing a vocabulary and an epistemic structure that, on the one hand, ends up imposing itself as "natural and objective," and on the other, builds itself on the same original matricide that it tries to bury. I do not expect every female reader to share my pleasure in undoing the Platonic fabric, but I hope that most will patiently follow my direction.

Chapter 2   The Maidservant from Thrace

1 Nothing tragic is envisioned here. The well is merely a cistern full of water where Thales unexpectedly took a bath.

2 One has only to consider how important "turning the soul away from the world of generation to the world of truth" (*Republic* 525c) is in Plato's definition of true philosophy. This "turning away" establishes a precise direction for the soul's inquiry, and hence for human thought. Pulling away from the realm of sensible and mutable things, thought must trun upward to contemplate the truth of the idea of the good. I have developed this argument in detail in a previous essay (Cavarero 1985: 289–321).

3 See, for example, Hannah Arendt (1978: 99–122).

4 It is Luce Irigaray's central thesis that philosophy, and hence society and culture, are founded on an ancient matricide (1993b: 18). I am convinced that the first philosophical text to contain this matricide is Parmenides' proem, an opinion that is shared by D.A. Conci (1989: 148–59).

5 Sometimes Greek scholars have pointed out that the terms of the

bipolar opposition man/woman correspond to the Greek *aner–gyne*, while *anthropos* designates the term man, understood as human species as distinct from animals. I think it is difficult to move beyond the oppositional logic of this kind of argument, because all the ancient texts at our disposal describe *anthropos* with masculine attributes. Since she is devoid of these attributes, woman is an *anthropos* of a lower level. We have only to consider Aristotle's political and rational *anthropos* as the paradigm according to which women are seen as lacking rationality, and hence are to be excluded from politics. For these reasons I maintain that current usage of the Italian term *uomo* [which translates into English as "man"] puts the argument in a nutshell.

6 See my own work on Hegel's interpretation of Parmenides (Cavarero 1984).

7 Plato's argument is a complex one and I will return to it later in order to illustrate briefly its basic passages. I would rather not deal with it in detail here, for fear of making this text too heavy. See two of my earlier works that articulate at greater length my understanding of Plato's so-called parricide (Cavarero 1976: 203–4; and 1988: 81–99).

8 According to Emanuele Severino, Greek philosophy established that the term "becoming" denotes the unavoidable passage from not-being to being, and vice versa, and so carries within it the sign of nothing. Hence the nihilistic destiny of Western philosophy as a philosophy in which nothing is inscribed in becoming. Supposedly, this destiny results from a misunderstanding of Parmenides' testimony, whose philosophical reflection revolves around the truth of being, a position that Severino supports (1982). I find it difficult to discuss my points of disagreement with Severino in a few lines while doing justice to his position. Nevertheless, I would like to note that in his recent writings Severino demonstrates the importance of the fear of death in the process through which the category of nothing has achieved its central status (1989). I do not share Severino's conclusions and his overall hermeneutical judgment, but I fully agree with his discussion of the meaning of *episteme* as a "remedy" for the fear of death.

9 For a more detailed analysis see my essay "Per una teoria della differenza sessuale" (1987).

10 The philosophical community Diotima dedicated a series of seminars to the theme of female realism, an important concept for the philosophy of sexual difference. These seminars have been published in Diotima, *Mettere al mondo il mondo*.

Chapter 3 Demeter

1 Bachofen is the best-known supporter of the thesis that the shift from matriarchy to patriarchy is based in history, rather than mythology or legend. However, he interprets the shift as the positive attainment of a superior civilization. This judgment formulated in 1861 has not softened in the past century. Rather, Bachofen's followers have confirmed its ideological foundation. For example, in one study published as late as 1982, we read: "matriarchy inexorably leads to the destruction of men, and therefore also to the impoverishment of women. Patriarchy alone grants women's freedom, understood as inseparable from men's freedom and from the freedom of the human race as a whole" (Devereux 1982: 276).

2 It is the daughter Kore who comes from darkness to light.

3 Everyday language perpetuates this crime, but only in part. For example, we say that a woman is expecting a baby (*bambino*). However, when the child is born we announce that it is either a baby boy (*bambino*) or a baby girl (*bambina*). It is significant that at least in the crucial moment of birth language does not sustain the universalization of the masculine. Here to say that a child is born means that either a girl or a boy is born, namely a definition is required and the masculine does not automatically stand for the feminine.

4 In this respect it is significant that the images we find on ancient Greek tombs are almost exclusively of men. It is an honor to have one's image passed on as a funerary effigy. But women appear to be worthy of being symbolized in death only if they died in childbirth, and in particular while giving birth to males (Keuls 1985: 138–44).

5 As is widely believed, when Andronicus was organizing books by Aristotle, he called for some to be placed on the shelf "after the books on physics" (*meta ta physica*). The modern sense of metaphysics developed from this, with the wider meaning of "above and beyond" physicality in the metaphorical as well as physical sense.

6 Significantly, one of the chapters of Page DuBois's *Sowing the Body* is entitled "The Oven." In the section called "Baking the Embryo" we read the following quotation from Hippocrates' treatise *The Nature of the Child* (12. 325): "As it inflates (in the womb), the seed forms a membrane around itself; for its surface, because of its viscosity, stretches around it without a break, in just the same way as a thin membrane is formed on the surface of bread when it is being baked; the bread rises as it grows warm and inflates,

and as it is inflated so the membraneous surface forms" (Du Bois 1988: 124).

7 Each country deals individually with its own demographic problems. Nonetheless, their global aspect is the world's overpopulation. This larger question is articulated around two central issues: (1) an imbalance of power between rich and poor countries where we find decreasing and increasing birth rates respectively; and (2) an enormous growth of hunger in the world, as a consequence of population growth in poor countries. Besides the typical "aid" of rich countries to poor countries, a preferred remedy is generally a politics directed toward decreasing birth rates in poor countries (sometimes even through sterilization). It is important to note that high birth rates are found in the cultures where patriarchal domination is strongest and least debated. In these cultures, maternal power, far from being actualized as a sovereign choice of female subjectivity, is merely a reproductive mechanism into which women are forced, first of all by culture and then also by nature.

8 Here a kind of manipulative visibility of the inside of a woman's womb replaces the visibility of the exterior of her swollen belly, which announces to the gaze that birth is rooted in her body and indeed does not "come from nothing."

9 The recent apostolic letter *Mulieris dignitatem* makes an effort to adopt the category of sexual difference. Nonetheless, it confirms the choice between mother and virgin as one to which the substance of female "value" is assigned. Not accidentally, both choices can be explained as functions of a kind of selfless dedication to service.

10 What is crucial here with respect to the usual model is that the daughter is a virgin for the mother, not for the man who can otherwise secure the possession of an intact, unviolated wife.

Chapter 4 Diotima

1 Although the majority of commentators claim that Diotima's speech is really that of Plato's Socrates, this does not exclude the possibility that a Mantinean priestess called Diotima may have in fact existed. For a defense of the position that Diotima's speech in the *Symposium* may be attributable to a historical personage, see Waithe 1991.

2 Luce Irigaray (1993a: 20–33) also observes this. Yet she suggests that in fact the speech can be considered as representing Diotima's own teaching, which may have occasionally lost some of its

coherence as the result of the interpolation of Socratic/Platonic thought.

3 Critics are quick to emphasize that Diotima's identity as a foreigner and as a priestess seems to suggest the mystical roots of Plato's teachings on Love. This may be true, but the symbolism is nonetheless polyvalent. It is only when analyzed from the standpoint of the feminist theory of sexual difference that this symbolism can open itself up to interpretations that otherwise remain lost or ambiguous.

4 Plato's passionate attachment to immortality, which is applied even to the physical cycle of generational succession, already suggests a vision in which birth is dialectically "saved" from blame. The most ancient patriarchal symbolism (repeated later in many guises) blames *birth* for generating living beings who are destined to die. In other words, it shifts the fear of death, a central category, onto birth, which is assumed as its *cause*. Bachofen provides an interesting analysis of the myth of Bellerophon. For Bachofen, Bellerophon is the hero who fights the Amazons and opposes the "law of the womb," since the womb gives birth to creatures destined to die, and offers nourishment only to death. Modern anthropologists have traced the tendency of blaming birth in many early cultures, where it appears as a kind of cliché that is coupled with the philosophical litany on coming from nothingness and going toward nothingness. See Burkert's thesis (1983) according to which man (the male human) kills animals and enemies, risking his own life to nurture and protect the new life generated by women. Here, the concept of guilty birth has become more sophisticated, so to speak. All humans born into the world are ultimately destined to die, but they need to be fed so that they do not die immediately, and men, as providers, must be prepared to risk their lives to ensure this.

5 See the following passages in Plato's *Theaetetus*: "My art of midwifery resembles the usual sort except in one way: the person giving birth is a man, not a woman, and souls, not bodies, are delivered" (150b). "Those who join in with me undergo the same experience as women giving birth: they have labor pains, and are troubled day and night with anxieties, even more so than pregnant women. My art has the power to arouse and to soothe these pains" (151a–b).

6 This seems to be the opinion of contemporary legal scholars for whom the preservation of one's own individual life (in Hobbes's terms the kind of power that provides the basic condition of all other power and is removed by death) is what inspires individuals to accept the social contract.

7 It is interesting to note in this regard how the hostility between men and animals (expressed in war as well as in hunting) recurs as a symbolic image throughout ancient texts. It is usually viewed by interpreters as something related to the need for humans to emphasize their indentity as different from the animal realm from which they originate (see G.A. Gilli 1988). The hostility between men and animals is in fact one of the basic elements of the masculine imprint that has attached itself to human identity. The divine link with animals through a female maternal brings to light a reversed symbolic order.

8 Although I have no statistical or scientific references to speak of, I cannot avoid noting something that has always struck me: the study of primates, especially the larger ones, seems often to have been pioneered by women. This must be inspired by a strong "calling," given how difficult it is for women to achieve scientific recognition, and especially given the fact that the study of primates must be carried out in their natural habitat, involving difficulty, danger, and physical stamina that stand in sharp contrast with traditional opinion of female behavior.

9 In this gaze directed back toward the past, the genetic history of animal life is obviously the closest to us, and it prompts us to look even farther back in order to embrace the Earth, which is represented in the feminine as "primordial motherhood" (Bachofen 1992: 123).

10 Cacciari would probably say no *ni-ente* (*no-thing*), coming from a hermeneutical perspective that is quite different from mine. Yet I think that we end up in the same place, agreeing on the "divine female contraction of the Past," though arriving there through different tortuous routes (Cacciari 1990: 518).

11 According to Muraro (1988: 66), this is "an extra-philosophical book, of a kind that is not to be found within the field of philosophy because it has been thrown out of it. This rejection did not happen yesterday. It happened a long time ago, although the book was published only in 1964 and was written probably a short time before that. The philosophy in the book is more ancient than that, and so is its expression."

12 See A. Morino's comment in the appendix to the Italian translation of Lispector's *A Paixão segundo G.H.* (Morino 1982: 167).

13 According to Simone Weil (1952: 97) "meditation on chance which led to the meeting of my father and mother is even more salutary than meditation on death. Is there a single thing in me of which the origin is not to be found in that meeting? Only God. And yet again, my thought of God had its origin in that meeting."

Bibliography

Translators' Note. We have designed this bibliography to serve the needs of an English-speaking readership. For modern works originally written in either French, German, or Portuguese, we cite both the original source and its English translation whenever possible. For ease of reference the first-named edition is that to which page references relate. We also list the Italian translation used by the author. For modern Italian works, we give the original reference and the English translation if one exists. For classical sources, we give a contemporary English translation.

Aeschylus, *Eumenides*, tr. A.J. Podlecki (Warminster: Aris & Phillips, 1987).
— *The Oresteia*, tr. Robert Fagles (New York: Viking, 1975).
Arendt, Hannah (1959): *The Human Condition*. New York: Doubleday. *Vita Activa; oder, Vom tätigen Leben* (Stuttgart: Kohlhammer, 1960). *Vita Activa*, tr. Sergio Finzi (Milan: Bompiani, 1988).
— (1978): *The Life of the Mind*, vol. 1: *Thinking*; and vol. 2: *Willing*. New York: Harcourt Brace Jovanovich. *La vita della mente*, tr. G. Zanetti (Bologna: Il Mulino, 1987).
Aristotle, *Metaphysics*, tr John H. McMahon (Buffalo: Prometheus, 1991).
— *Politics*, tr. Carnes Lord. (Chicago: University of Chicago Press, 1984).

Bachofen, John Jacob (1992) *Myth, Religion and Mother Right: Selected Writings by J.J. Bachofen*, tr. Ralph Manheim. Princeton: Princeton University Press. Das Mutterrecht (Stuttgart: Krais & Hoffman, 1861). *Il matriarcato*, tr. Furio Iesi and Giulio Schiavoni (Turin: Einaudi, 1988).

Blumenberg, Hans (1987): *Das Lachen der Thrakerin: Eine Urgeschichte der Theorie*. Frankfurt am Main: Suhrkamp.

Bock, Gisela (1992): "Equality and Difference in National Social Racism." In Gisela Bock and Susan James (eds), *Beyond Equality and Difference: citizenship, feminist politics, and female subjectivity*. London and New York: Routledge.

Burkert, Walter (1983): *Homo Necans: The Anthropology of Ancient Greek Sacrificial Ritual and Myth*, tr. Peter Bing. Berkeley: University of California Press, 1983. *Homo necans: Interpretationen altgriechischer Opferriten und Mythen* (Berlin and New York: De Gruyter, 1972). *Homo Necans*, tr. F. Bertolini (Turin: Boringhieri, 1981).

Cacciari, Massimo (1990): *Dell'Inizio*. Milan: Adelphi.

Cavarero, Adriana (1976): *Dialettica e politica in Platone*. Padua: CEDAM.

—— (1984): *L'interpretazione hegeliana di Parmenide*. Trento: Pubblicazione di Verifiche 10.

—— (1985): "Il bene nella filosofia politica di Platone e di Aristotele." *Filosofia Politica*, 2.

—— (1987): "Per una teoria della differenza sessuale." In Diotima, *Il pensiero della differenza sessuale*. Milan: La Tartaruga.

—— (1988): "Platone e Hegel interpreti di Parmenide." *La parola del passato*, 43, 81–99.

—— (1990): "Dire la nascita." In Diotima, *Metters al mondo il mondo*. Milan: La Tartaruga, 1990.

Conci, D.A. (1989): "Il matricidio filosofico occidentale: Parmenide di Elea." In Tilde Giani Gallino (ed.), *Le Grandi Madri*. Milan: Feltrinelli.

Dante (1966): *Inferno* (in Italian and English), tr. Ronald Bottrall, ed. Terence Tiller. New York: Schocken.

Del Re, Alisia (1989): "Politiche demografiche e controllo sociale in Francia, Italia e Germania negli anni'30." In *Stato e rapporti sociali di sesso* [various authors]. Milan: Angeli.

Devereux, George (1982): *Femme et mythe*. Paris: Flammarion. *Donna e mito*, tr. Mariangela Zanusso (Milan: Feltrinelli, 1984).

Diotima [Collective Authorship] (1990): *Mettere al mondo il mondo*. Milan: La Tartaruga, 1990.

DuBois, Page (1988): *Sowing the Body: psychoanalysis and ancient representations of women*. University Chicago of Press, 1988. *Il corpo come metafora* (Rome and Bari: Laterza, 1990).

Euripides, *The Bacchae*, tr. Donald Sutherland (Lincoln: University of Nebraska Press, 1968).

Fattorini, Emma (1987): "Del divino biologico." *Reti*, 2.

Giani Gallino, Tilde (ed.) (1989): *Le Grandi Madri*. Milan: Feltrinelli.

Gilli, G.A. (1988): *Origini dell'eguaglianza. Ricerche sociologiche sull'antica Grecia*. Turin: Einaudi.

Habermas, Jürgen (1987): *The Theory of Communicative Action*, vol. 2: *Lifeworld and System: a critique of functionalist reason*, tr. Thomas McCarthy. Boston: Beacon Press. *Theorie des Kommunikativen Handelns* (Frankfurt am Main: Suhrkamp, 1981). *Teoria dell'agire comunicativo* (Bologna: Il Mulino, 1986).

Hegel, G.W.F. (1969): *Hegel's Science of Logic*, tr. Arnold V. Miller. London: Allen & Unwin. *Wissenschaft der Logik* (Hamburg: Meiner, 1963). *Scienza della logica*, tr. Antonio Moni (Bari: Laterza, 1984).

Hippocrates: "The Nature of the Child." In Iain M. Lonie, *The Hippocratic Treatises: a commentary* (Berlin and New York, Gruyter, 1981).

Homer, *Odyssey*, tr. Robert Fitzgerald (New York: Doubleday 1961).

Ipazia. Quattro venerdì e un giovedì per la filosofia [various authors) (1988): Milan: Edizioni di Via Dogana.

Irigaray, Luce (1993a): *Ethics of Sexual Difference*, tr. Carolyn Burke and Gillan C. Gill. Ithaca, NY: Cornell University Press. *L'Etique de la différence sexuelle* (Paris: Minuit, 1984). *Etica della differenza sessuale*, tr. Luisa Muraro and Antonella Leoni (Milan: Feltrinelli, 1985).

—— (1993b): *Sexes and Genealogies*, tr. Gillian C. Gill. New York: Columbia University Press. *Sexes et parentés* (Paris: Minuit, 1987).

Kaufmann, Arthur (1990): "Verscharfen oder Strichen?", Interviewer Brigitte Schwartz. *Die Zeit*, 8 (Feb. 16).

Keuls, Eva C. (1985): *The Reign of the Phallus: Sexual Politics in Ancient Athens*. New York: Harper & Row. *Il regno della fallocrazia*, tr. M. Carpi (Milan: Il Saggiatore, 1988).

Lispector, Clarice (1984): *Family Ties*, tr. Giovanni Pontiero. Austin: University of Texas Press. *Laços de Família* (Rio de Janeiro: Livraria J. Olympio Editora, 1960; 1982). *Legami familiari*, tr. Adelina Aletti (Milan: Feltrinelli, 1986).

—— (1988): *The Passion according to G.H.*, tr. Ronald W. Sousa. Minneapolis: University of Minnesota Press. *A Paixão segundo G.H.*

(Rio de Janeiro: Sabiá, 1968). La passione secondo G.H., tr. Adelina Aletti (Turin: La Rosa, 1982).

Mancina, Claudia (1987): "Bioetica, il campo di un conflitto." *Reti*, 1.

Morino, A. (1982): "Afterword." In Clarice Lispector, *La passione secondo G.H.* Turin: La Rosa.

Muraro, Luisa (1988): "Commento alla *Passione secondo G.H.*" *DonnaWomanFemme (DWF)*, 5/6.

Otto, Walter F. (1965): *Dionysus: Myth and Cult*, tr. Robert B. Palmer. Bloomington: Indiana University Press. *Dionysus: Mythos und Kultus* (Frankfurt: Klostermann, 1933). *Dionisio.* tr. Albina Ferretti Calenda (Genoa: Il Melangolo, 1990).

Parmenides, *Fragments*, in *Parmenides: A Text with Translation, Commentary, and Critical Essays*, ed. L. Tarán (Princeton: Princeton University Press, 1965).

Plato, *Cratylus, Parmenides, Greater Hippias, Lesser Hippias*, tr. H.N. Fowler. (Cambridge, Mass.: Harvard University Press, 1977).

— *Ion*, tr. J.M. MacGregor (Cambridge: Cambridge University Press, 1912; repr. 1956).

— *Phaedo*, tr. David Gallop (Oxford: Clarendon Press, 1975).

— *The Republic*, tr. G.M.A. Grube (Indianapolis and Cambridge: Hackett, 1992).

— *Symposium*, tr. W. Hamilton (Melbourne: Penguin, 1952).

— *Theaetetus*, in Francis M. Cornford, *Plato's Theory of Knowledge* (New York; Liberal Arts Press, 1957).

Putino, Angela (1988): "Donna Guerriera." *DonnaWomanFemme (DWF)*, 7.

Sassi, Maria Michela (1988): *La scienza dell'uomo nell'antica Grecia.* Turin: Boringhieri.

Severino, Emanuele (1982): "Ritornare a Parmenide." In *Essenza del nichilismo.* Milan: Adelphi.

— (1989): *Il giogo.* Milan: Adelphi.

Sissa, Giulia (1983): "Il corpo della donna. Lineamenti di una ginecologia filosofica. In Silva Campese, Paola Manuli, and Giulia Sissa, *Madre materia.* Turin: Boringhieri.

Snell, Bruno (1960): *The Discovery of the Mind: The Greek Origins of European Thought*, tr. T.G. Rosenmeyer. New York: Harper. *Die Entdeckung des Geistes: Studien zur Entstehung des europais-chen Denkens bei den Griechen* (Hamburg: Claassen & Goverts, 1948). *La culture greca e le origini del pensiero europeo*, tr. Vera Degli Alberti and Anna Solmi Marietti (Turin: Einaudi, 1963).

Tarozzi, Bianca (1989): "Variazioni sul tema di Penelope." In *Nessuno vince il leone*. Venice: Arsenale.

Traverso, Carlo Emilio (1977): *La tutela costituzionale della persona umana prima della nascita*. Milan: A. Giuffré.

Vegetti Finzi, Silvia (1987): "Corpi e menti in sintonia." *Reti*, 1.

Waithe, Mary Ellen (1991): "Diotima of Mantinea." In *A History of Women Philosophers*, vol. 1: 83–116. Dordrecht: Martinus Nijhoff.

Weil, Simone (1952): *Gravity and Grace*, tr. Emma Craufurd. London: Routledge. *La pesanteur et la grâce (Paris: Plon, 1948). L'ombra della grazia* (Milan: Rusconi, 1985).

Index

www.ingramcontent.com/pod-product-compliance
Ingram Content Group UK Ltd.
Pitfield, Milton Keynes, MK11 3LW, UK
UKHW022016120125
453522UK00015B/431